candycrochet

50 adorable designs for infants & toddlers

candi jensen

candy crochet

50 adorable designs for infants & toddlers

candi jensen

sixth&spring books

sixth&spring books
233 Spring Street
New York, New York, 10013

Vice President, Publisher
Trisha Malcolm

Editorial Director
Elaine Silverstein

Art Director
Chi Ling Moy

Graphic Designers
Kim Howie
Sheena T. Paul

Book Division Manager
Erica Smith

Associate Editor
Erin Walsh

Yarn Editors
Tanis Gray
Veronica Manno

Instructions Editors
Rita Greenfeder
Pat Harste
Carla Scott

Writer
Daryl Brower

Copy Editors
Wendy R. Preston
Kristina Sigler

Technical Illustrations
Uli Mönch

Production Manager
David Joinnides

**President and Publisher,
Sixth&Spring Books**
Art Joinnides

Photography: Dan Howell

1 3 5 7 9 10 8 6 4 2

Manufactured in China

Library of Congress Control Number: 2006931203

ISBN-10: 1-933027-17-7

ISBN-13: 978-1-933027-17-3

contents

introduction 7
sweaters & vests 8-55

preppy preschooler · berry pretty · poncho power
fringed benefit · flower power · vest friend
pretty in pink · party princess · versatile vest
highland charm · in the navy · hippie chic

chill chasers 56-95

fur real · pompom panache · feet first
spice girl · pastel parfait · fur ever
square toppers · golden child · hot step
raspberry rhapsody

sets 96-127

emerald isle · summer love · tank girl
fine lines · ahoy, matey! · east meets west
warm front

dresses 128-139

simply mauve-olous · cross my heart · holiday magic

blankies 140-193

nursery magic · bear necessity · tickled pink · peewee pizzazz
jean dream · purr-fection · english beat · pattern play
cowboy blues · farm fresh · ripple effect · navajo throw
creature comfort · square dance · blue marine · true blue

basics 194-198
size chart 199
resources 200

introduction

When I was a child, my mom was always busy sewing clothes for my sisters and me, and she dressed us alike as if we were triplets. Mom had a wonderful eye for color and style and could whip something up just by looking at a picture. Although I have never been as skilled at sewing as my mom, I was able to carry on her legacy through knitting and crochet.

After I had my own children, I was inspired to make them one-of-a-kind sweaters that always made them stand out on the playground. It was the early '70s, when anything was possible and color, texture and especially crochet were in fashion. Although my children are now grown, my grandchildren—Veronica, Johnny, and the newest, Charlie—are a great source of inspiration.

I'm still a sucker for a girly little sweater, but the boys have challenged me to think of garments that are appropriate for them. When Johnny was still very young, he would call me up and say, "Must see Grandma!" I would have offered to buy him a new car after one of those calls, but I settled for making him a sweater. As he and the other grandbabies started to grow out of the clothes that I lovingly made for them, I would try to squeeze them into sweaters that probably showed way too much belly. Then I realized that their growth spurts could be an excuse to design yet more garments for them.

As you look at the designs in this book, I hope you'll find something to make for the special little ones in your life. Though they'll undoubtedly grow out of it, you can always "just make more."

Candi Jensen

preppy preschooler

Cheerful stripes and minimal shaping make this no-fuss project a breeze to crochet! Worked in an ultra-plush, fleece-like yarn, this transseasonal favorite will keep your wee one stylishly warm all year long.

SIZES

Instructions are written for size 3–6 months. Changes for sizes 9–12 months, 18–24 months and 3 years are in parentheses.

FINISHED MEASUREMENTS

- Chest 22 (24, 26, 28)"/56 (61, 66, 71)cm
- Length 11 (12, 14, 15)"/28 (30.5, 35.5, 38)cm
- Upper arm 9 (10, 11, 12)"/23 (25.5, 28, 30.5)cm

MATERIALS

ORIGINAL YARN

- *4 (5, 5, 6) 1¾oz/50g balls (each approx 114yd/104m) of Wendy/Berroco, Inc.'s* ***Velvet Touch*** *(nylon) in #2051 amethyst (MC)* (4)
- *1 ball in #1204 lime velvet (CC)*

SUBSTITUTE YARN

- *7 (8, 8, 10) 1¾oz/50g balls (each approx 74yd/68m) of Cleckheaton's* ***Deluxe Velvet Ribbon*** *(nylon/acrylic) in #014 blue (MC)* (4)
- *1 ball in #001 lime (CC)*
- *Size H/8 (5mm) crochet hook or size to obtain gauge*
- *1 set of markers*

GAUGE

12 sts and 10 rows to 4"/10cm over hdc using size H/8 (5mm) hook.

Take time to check gauge.

NOTE

See page 194 for how to make color changes.

BACK

With MC, ch 36 (38, 42, 44).

Foundation row Hdc in 3rd ch from hook and in each ch across—34 (36, 40, 42) sts. Join CC, ch 2, turn.

Row 2 Hdc in each st across. Ch 2, turn. Working in hdc, work in stripe pat as foll: 1 row CC, 2 rows MC, 2 rows CC, 1 row MC and 1 row CC. Join MC, ch 2, turn. Work even until piece measures 11 (12, 14, 15)"/28 (30.5, 35.5, 38)cm from beg. Fasten off.

FRONT

Work as for back until piece measures 7 (7½, 9, 9½)"/17.5 (19, 23, 24)cm from beg. Ch 2, turn.

Left neck shaping

Next row Work across first 16 (17, 19, 20) sts. Ch 2, turn. Dec 1 st from neck edge every other row 5 (6, 6, 7) times—11 (11, 13, 13) sts. Work even until same length as back. Fasten off.

Right neck shaping

Next row Sk 2 center sts, join yarn with a hdc in next st, work to end. Cont to work as for left neck, reversing shaping.

SLEEVES

With MC, ch 20 (22, 24, 24).

Foundation row Hdc in 3rd ch from hook and in each ch across—18 (20, 22, 22) sts. Join CC, ch 2, turn. Working in hdc, work in stripe pat as foll: 2 rows CC, 1 row MC, 1 row CC, 2 rows MC and 1 row CC; then work with MC only, AT SAME TIME, inc 1 st each side every other row 3 times, every 4th row 2 (2, 3, 4) times—28 (30, 34, 36) sts. Work even until piece measures 7½ (8, 9, 10)"/19 (20, 23, 25.5)cm from beg. Fasten off.

FINISHING

Sew shoulder seams.

Neck edging

From RS, join CC with a sl st in left shoulder seam.

Rnd 1 Ch 1, making sure that work lies flat, sc around neck edge, dec 1 st over 2 center sts. Join rnd with a sl st in ch-1 changing to MC.

Rnd 2 Sc in each st around, dec 1 st over 2 center sts. Join rnd with a sl st in ch-1. Fasten off. Place markers 4½ (5, 5½, 6)"/11.5 (12.5, 14, 15)cm down from shoulder seams on front and back. Sew sleeves to armholes between markers. Sew side and sleeve seams.

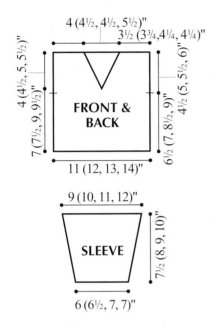

Front & Back: 4 (4½, 4½, 5½)" / 3½ (3¾, 4¼, 4¼)" / 4 (4½, 5, 5½)" / 7 (7½, 9, 9½)" / 6½ (7, 8½, 9)" / 4½ (5, 5½, 6)" / 11 (12, 13, 14)"

Sleeve: 9 (10, 11, 12)" / 7½ (8, 9, 10)" / 6 (6½, 7, 7)"

Mix it up a little—sensational half double crochet stripes, vibrant granny squares and whimsical fringe add up to fun in this retro V-neck pullover. It offers nonstop versatility for a hip little miss who likes to dress to impress.

fringed benefit

SIZES

Instructions are written for size 3–6 months. Changes for sizes 12–24 months and 3 years are in parentheses.

FINISHED MEASUREMENTS

• Chest 20 (25, 30)"/51 (63.5, 76)cm

• Length 11 (13, 15)"/28 (33, 38)cm
(not including tassels)

• Upper arm 8 (10, 12)"/20 (25.5, 30.5)cm

MATERIALS

ORIGINAL YARN

• 2 (2, 3) 1¾oz/50g balls (each approx 131yd/120m) of Knit One, Crochet Too's **Creme Brulee** (wool) in #235 deep plum (A) (3)

• 1 ball each in #789 violet (B), #620 powder blue (C), #527 kiwi (D) and #513 key lime (E)

SUBSTITUTE YARN

• 3 (3, 4) 1¾oz/50g balls (each approx 105yd/96m) of Cleckheaton/Plymouth Yarn's **Country 8 Ply** (wool) in #2160 raspberry (A) (3)

• 1 ball each in #2246 lilac (B), #2280 blue (C), #2250 lime (D) and #2234 pale yellow (E)

• Size G/6 (4mm) crochet hook or size to obtain gauges

• 3¼ x 3¼"/8 x 8cm piece of cardboard (for tassels)

• 1 set of markers

GAUGES

• 16 sts and 13 rows to 4"/10cm over hdc using size G/6 (4mm) hook.

• One square to 5"/12.5cm using size G/6 (4mm) hook.

Take time to check gauges.

NOTES

1 See page 196 for granny square basics.

2 See page 194 for how to make color changes.

STRIPE PATTERN

Work 1 row each C, D, E, A and B.

Rep these 5 rows for stripe pat.

BACK

With A, ch 42 (52, 62).

Row 1 Hdc in 3rd ch from hook and in each ch across—40 (50, 60) sts. Join B, ch 2, turn.

Row 2 Hdc in each st across. Join C, ch 2, turn. Cont in hdc and in stripe pat, and work even until piece measures 6 (8, 10)"/15 (20, 25.5)cm from beg. Fasten off.

FRONT

Work as for back until piece measures 2½ (4, 5½)"/6 (10, 14)cm from beg.

Left neck shaping

Next row Work across 19 (24, 29) sts, join next color, ch 2, turn. Dec 1 st from neck edge every row 6 (7, 9) times—13 (17, 20) sts. Work even until same length as back. Fasten off.

Right neck shaping

Next row Sk 2 center sts, join next color with a hdc in next st, work to end. Cont to work as for left neck, reversing shaping.

SLEEVES

With A, ch 26 (30, 34).

Row 1 Hdc in 3rd ch from hook and in each ch across—24 (28, 32) sts. Join B, ch 2, turn.

Row 2 Hdc in each st across. Join C, ch 2, turn. Cont in hdc and stripe pat, AT SAME TIME, inc 1 st each side every other row 4 (6, 8) times—32 (40, 48) sts. Work even until piece measures 6 (8, 9)"/15 (20, 23)cm from beg. Fasten off.

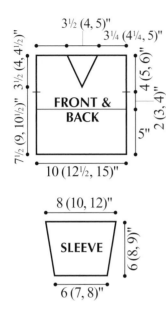

3½ (4, 5)"
3¼ (4¼, 5)"

7½ (9, 10½)"   3½ (4, 4½)"

FRONT & BACK

4 (5, 6)"

2 (3, 4)"

5"

10 (12½, 15)"

8 (10, 12)"

SLEEVE

6 (8, 9)"

6 (7, 8)"

GRANNY SQUARES

Make 4 (5, 6). Work as for multicolor basic granny square working rnd 1 with E, rnd 2 with D, rnd 3 with C, rnd 4 with B and rnd 5 with A.

FINISHING

Sew shoulder seams. Place markers 4 (5, 6)"/10 (12.5, 15)cm down from shoulder seams on front and back. Sew sleeves to armholes between markers. Sew side and sleeve seams. Sew squares tog forming a ring.

For sizes 3–6 months and 3 years only

Sew squares to bottom edge of front and back, matching side seams.

For size 12–24 months only

Sew squares to bottom edge of front and back, positioning a square at center front.

Neck edging

From RS, join A with a sl st in left shoulder seam.

Rnd 1 Ch 1, making sure that work lies flat, sc around neck edge, dec 1 st over center 2 sts. Join rnd with a sl st in ch-1. Fasten off.

Tassels

Make 20 (25, 30). Wrap A 11 times around cardboard. Slip a 10"/25.5cm-length of A under strands and tightly knot at one end of cardboard. Remove cardboard. Wrap and tie another length of yarn around the tassel about ¾"/2cm down from the top. Cut loops at opposite ends. Trim ends even. Sew tassels around bottom edge, as shown.

Put a new spin on tradition: A sugary confection to crochet, this sweet V-neck pullover in a fanciful argyle pattern features stripes along the back, chain stitch crosses and decorative bobbles on the sleeves.

pretty in pink

Instructions are written for size 3–6 months.

Changes for sizes 9–12 months, 18–24 months and 3 years are in parentheses.

FINISHED MEASUREMENTS

- Chest 22 (24, 26, 28)"/56 (61, 66, 71)cm
- Length 12 (13, 14, 15)"/30.5 (33, 35.5, 38)cm
- Upper arm 9 (10, 11, 12)"/23 (25.5, 28, 30.5)cm

MATERIALS

- *3 (4, 4, 5) 1¾oz/50g balls (each approx 136yd/124m) of Patons' **Grace** (mercerized cotton) in #60416 blush (A)* **3**
- *2 balls in #60437 rose (B)*
- *1 ball each in #60450 coral (C), #60409 ruby (D) and #60322 viola (E)*
- *Size G/6 (4mm) crochet hook or size to obtain gauge*
- *11 bobbins*

NOTE

One of the original colors used for this sweater is no longer available. The following substitution is recommended:

- *#60604 terracotta for #60450 coral (C)*

GAUGE

20 sts and 20 rows to 4"/10cm over pat st using size G/6 (4mm) hook.

Take time to check gauge.

NOTES

1 See page 195 for how to work color changes for argyle patterns.

2 Wind A onto 5 bobbins, and C and D onto 3 bobbins each.

3 See page 194 for how to work color changes for rows.

4 See page 196 for how to embroider chain stitch.

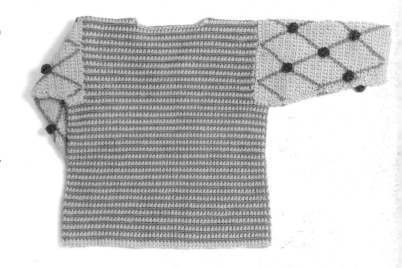

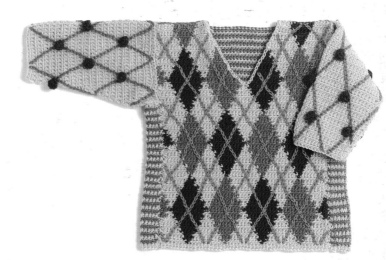

Row 1 Sc in back lp of each st across. Ch 1, turn. Rep row 1 for pat st.

STRIPE PATTERN

Working in pat st, work 1 row B and 1 row A. Rep these 2 rows for stripe pat.

BACK

With A, ch 67 (73, 83, 87). **Foundation row** Sc in 2nd ch from hook and in each ch across—66 (72, 82, 86) sts. Change to B, ch 1, turn. Cont in pat st and stripe pat and work even until piece measures 7½ (8, 8½, 9)"/19 (20, 21.5, 23)cm from beg. Fasten off. Turn work.

Armhole shaping

Next row Keeping to stripe pat, sk first 10 (10, 15, 15) sts, join next color with a sc in next st, work across to within last 10 (10, 15, 15) sts. Join next color, ch 1, turn—46 (52, 52, 56) sts. Work even until piece measures 12 (13, 14, 15)"/30.5 (33, 35.5, 38)cm from beg. Fasten off.

FRONT

With A, ch 47 (53, 53, 57). **Foundation row** Sc in 2nd ch from hook and in ch across—46 (52, 52, 56) sts. Ch 1, turn. Cont in pat st.

Beg chart

Row 11 (7, 7, 1) Beg with st 6 (3, 3, 1) and work to st 51 (54, 54, 56). Cont to foll chart in this way until row 52 is completed.

Left neck shaping

Row 53 (RS) Work across first 22 (25, 25, 27) sts, ch 1 turn. Dec 1 st from neck edge every row 6 times, every other row 2 (4, 4, 5) times—14 (15, 15, 16) sts. Work even until row 69 (71, 73, 75) is completed. Fasten off.

Color Key

☐ Blush (A)

▨ Coral (C)

■ Ruby (D)

⊡ Viola (E) Chain st

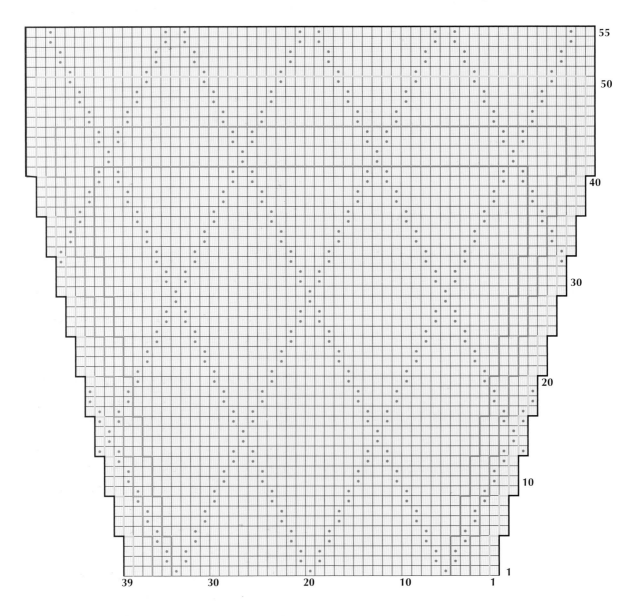

55

50

40

30

20

10

1

39   30   20   10   1

Color Key

☐ Blush (A)

⊡ Viola (E) Chain st

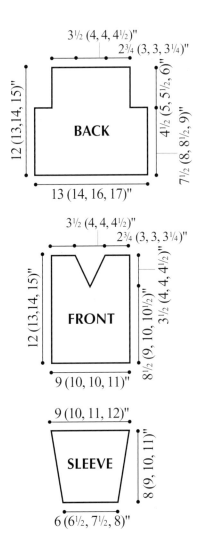

3½ (4, 4, 4½)"

2¾ (3, 3, 3¼)"

12 (13, 14, 15)"

4½ (5, 5½, 6)"

BACK

7½ (8, 8½, 9)"

13 (14, 16, 17)"

3½ (4, 4, 4½)"

2¾ (3, 3, 3¼)"

12 (13, 14, 15)"

3½ (4, 4, 4½)"

FRONT

8½ (9, 10, 10½)"

9 (10, 10, 11)"

9 (10, 11, 12)"

SLEEVE

8 (9, 10, 11)"

6 (6½, 7½, 8)"

Right neck shaping

Row 53 (RS) Keeping to chart pat, sk 2 center sts, join yarn with a sc in next st, work to end. Cont to work as for left neck, reversing shaping.

SLEEVES

With A, ch 30 (34, 38, 40). **Foundation row** Sc in 2nd ch from hook and in each ch across—29 (33, 37, 39) sts. Ch 1, turn. Cont in pat st, AT SAME TIME, inc 1 st each side every 4th row 8 (10, 10, 10) times—45 (53, 57, 59) sts. Work even until piece measures 8 (9, 10, 11)"/20 (23, 25.5, 28)cm from beg. Fasten off.

FINISHING

Embroidery

Referring to chart for front, use E to embroider chain-stitch diagonal lines. Referring to chart for sleeves, use B to embroider chain stitch diagonal lines.

Bobbles

Make 10 (18, 18, 18). With D, ch 2 leaving a long tail for sewing. **Row 1** In 2nd ch from hook work [yo, draw up a lp, yo, draw through 2 lps on hook] 4 times, yo and draw through all 5 lps on hook. Fasten off leaving a long tail for sewing. On each sleeve, sew a bobble where diagonal lines intersect. Sew shoulder and side seams. Set in sleeves, sewing last 1(1, 1½, 1½)"/2.5 (2.5, 4, 4)cm at top of sleeve to armhole sts. Sew sleeve seams.

Neck edging

From RS, join A with a sl st in left shoulder seam.

Rnd 1 Ch 1, making sure that work lies flat, sc around neck edge, dec 1 st over 2 sts at beg of neck shaping. Join rnd with a sl st in ch-1. Fasten off.

aired with a T-shirt and jeans, this take-everywhere cardigan is an urban essential. Color-blocked sleeves and front body are complemented by a richly striped back, while a bold argyle motif adds dynamic interest.

highland charm

SIZES

Instructions are written for size 3–6 months. Changes for sizes 9–12 months, 18–24 months and 3 years are in parentheses.

FINISHED MEASUREMENTS

- Chest (buttoned) 22 (24, 26, 28)"/56 (61, 66, 71)cm
- Length 12 (13, 14, 15)"/30.5 (33, 35.5, 38)cm
- Upper arm 9 (10, 11, 12)"/23 (25.5, 28, 30.5)cm

MATERIALS

ORIGINAL YARN

- 2 1¾oz/50g balls (each approx 138yd/ 126m) of Classic Elite Yarns' **Waterspun** (wool) in #5035 lime green (A) 4
- 1 ball each in #5049 blue (B), #5050 olive green (C), #5046 teal blue (D), #5027 red purple (E) and #5068 orange (F)

SUBSTITUTE YARN

- 3 1¾oz/50g balls (each approx 110yd/100m) of Classic Elite Yarns' **Renaissance** (wool) in #7135 celery (A) 4
- 2 balls each in #7104 lapis (B), #7172 green pepper (C), #7146 alpine spruce (D), #7127 chianti (E) and #7178 tiled roof (F)
- Size H/8 (5mm) crochet hook or size to obtain gauge
- 9 bobbins
- 4 (4, 5, 5) ¾"/19mm buttons

GAUGE

16 sts and 16 rows to 4"/10cm over pat st using size H/8 (5mm) hook.
Take time to check gauge.

NOTES

1 See page 195 for how to work color changes for argyle patterns.
2 Wind A onto 2 bobbins and B, C, D and E onto separate bobbins.
3 See page 194 for how to work color changes for rows.
4 See page 196 for how to embroider chain stitch.

PATTERN STITCH

Row 1 Sc in back lp of each st across. Ch 1, turn. Rep row 1 for pat st.

STRIPE PATTERN

Working in pat st, work 1 row each B, C, D, E, F and A. Rep these 6 rows for stripe pat.

BACK

With A, ch 53 (57, 65, 69). **Foundation row** Sc in 2nd ch from hook and in each ch across—52 (56, 64, 68) sts. Join B, ch 1, turn. Cont in pat st and stripe pat and work even until piece measures 7½ (8, 8½, 9)"/19 (20, 21.5, 23)cm from beg. Fasten off. Turn work.

Armhole shaping

Next row Keeping to stripe pat, sk first 8 (8, 12, 12) sts, join next color with a sc in next st, work across to within last 8 (8, 12, 12) sts. Join next color, ch 1, turn—36 (40, 40, 44) sts. Work even until piece measures 12 (13, 14,15)"/30.5 (33, 35.5, 38)cm from beg. Fasten off.

LEFT FRONT

With A, ch 18 (20, 20, 22). **Foundation row (WS)** Sc in 2nd ch from hook and in each ch across—17 (19, 19, 21) sts. Ch 1, turn. Cont in pat st.

Beg chart 1

Row 7 (5, 3, 1) Beg with st 3 (2, 2, 1) and work to st 19 (20, 20, 21). Cont to foll chart in this way until row 40 is completed.

Neck shaping

Row 41 (RS) Work across to within last 2 sts, dec 1 st over last 2 sts. Cont to dec 1 st from neck edge every row 3 (4, 4, 5) times more, every other row 4 times—9 (10, 10, 11) sts. Work even until row 54 (56, 58, 60) is completed. Fasten off.

RIGHT FRONT

Work as for left front, foll chart 2 and reversing neck shaping.

LEFT SLEEVE

With E, ch 25 (29, 31, 33). **Foundation row** Sc in 2nd ch from hook and in each ch across—24 (28, 30, 32) sts. Cont in pat st and inc 1 st each side every 4th row 6 (6, 7, 8) times—36 (40, 44, 48) sts. Work even until piece measures 8 (9, 10, 11)"/20 (23, 25.5, 28)cm from beg. Fasten off.

RIGHT SLEEVE

Work as for left sleeve using B.

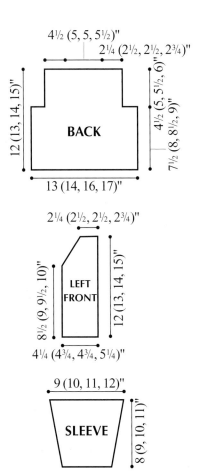

4½ (5, 5, 5½)"

2¼ (2½, 2½, 2¾)"

12 (13, 14, 15)"

BACK

4½ (5, 5½, 6)"

7½ (8, 8½, 9)"

13 (14, 16, 17)"

2¼ (2½, 2½, 2¾)"

8½ (9, 9½, 10)"

LEFT FRONT

12 (13, 14, 15)"

4¼ (4¾, 4¾, 5¼)"

9 (10, 11, 12)"

SLEEVE

8 (9, 10, 11)"

6 (7, 7½, 8)"

FINISHING

Embroidery

Referring to charts 1 and 2, use F to embroider chain-stitch diagonal lines on fronts. Referring to chart 3, use A to embroider chain-stitch diagonal lines on sleeves. Sew shoulder and side seams. Set in sleeves, sewing last 1 (1, 1½, 1½)"/2.5 (2.5, 4, 4)cm at top of sleeve to armhole sts. Sew sleeve seams.

Edging

From RS, join F with a sl st in left side seam. **Rnd 1** Ch 1, making sure that work lies flat, sc around entire edge, working 3 sc in each corner. Join rnd with a sl st in ch-1. Fasten off.

Button band

With RS facing and F, join yarn with a sc in first st at bottom edge of right front. Sc in each st to beg of neck shaping. Ch 1, turn. Work 1 row even. Fasten off. Place markers on band for 4 (4, 5, 5) buttons, with the first ¾"/2cm from beg of neck shaping, the last 1¼"/3cm from bottom edge and the rest spaced evenly between.

Buttonhole band

With RS facing and F, join yarn with a sc in first st at beg of neck shaping of left front. **Buttonhole row** *Sc to marker, ch 2, sk next 2 sts; rep from * to first st at bottom edge. Ch 1, turn. **Next row** Sc in each st and work 2 sc in each ch-2 sp across. Fasten off. Sew on buttons.

Chart 2

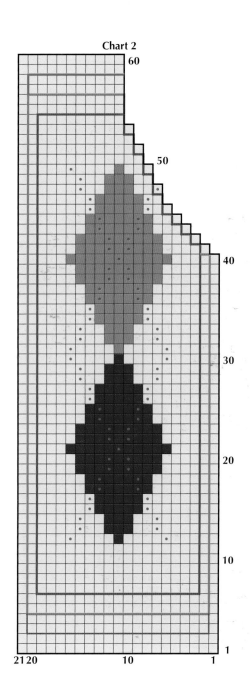

Chart 1

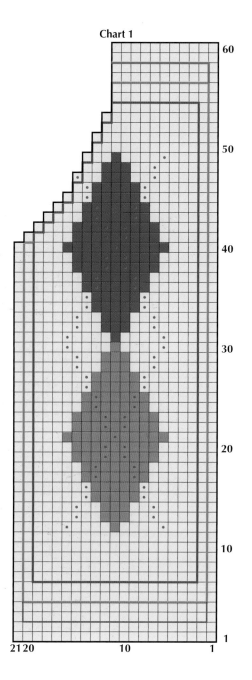

Color Key

- ☐ Lime (A)
- ▨ Blue (B)
- ▨ Olive (C)
- ▨ Teal blue (D)
- ■ Red purple (E)
- ⊡ Orange (F) chain st

Color Key

■ Red purple (E)

▪ Lime (A) chain st

Chart 3

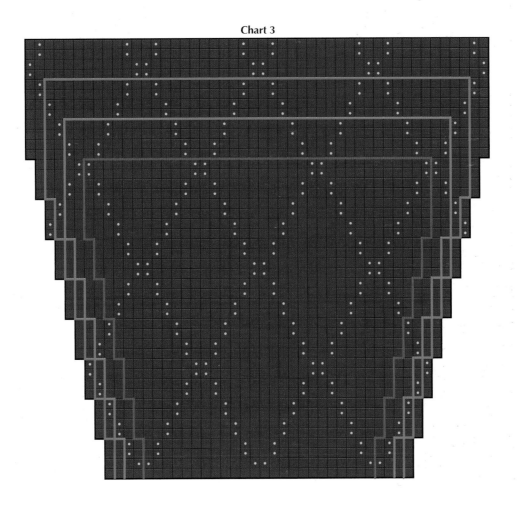

When ease and comfort are the order of the day, your small fry can relax in this delightful basic pullover. Subtly shaded ribbon yarn provides ample texture and dramatic color interest; a simple shell stitch–edged collar and striking silk violets add touches of elegance.

berry pretty

SIZES

Instructions are written for size 3–6 months.
Changes for sizes 9–12 months, 18–24 months and
3 years are in parentheses.

FINISHED MEASUREMENTS

- Chest 22 (24, 26, 28)"/56 (61, 66, 71)cm
- Length 11 (12, 13, 14)"/28 (30.5, 33, 35.5)cm
- Upper arm 9 (10, 11, 12)"/23 (25.5, 28, 30.5)cm

MATERIALS

- *6 (8, 9, 10) 1¾oz/50g balls (each approx*
75yd/69m) of Knit One, Crochet Too's **Tartelette**
(cotton/nylon) in #235 raspberry 🧶4
- *Size J/10 (6mm) crochet hook or size to obtain gauge*
- *1 set of markers*

GAUGE

11 sts and 8 rows to 4"/10cm over hdc
using size J/10 (6mm) hook.
Take time to check gauge.

BACK

Ch 32 (36, 38, 40).

Row 1 (WS) Hdc in 3rd ch from hook and in each ch across—30 (34, 36, 38) sts. Ch 2, turn.

Row 2 Hdc in each st across. Ch 2, turn. Rep row 2 for pat st and work even until piece measures 11 (12, 13, 14)"/28 (30.5, 33, 35.5)cm from beg. Fasten off.

FRONT

Work as for back until piece measures 7½ (8, 8½, 9)"/19 (20, 21.5, 23)cm from beg, end with a WS row.

Left neck shaping

Next row (RS) Work across first 14 (16, 17, 18) sts, ch 2, turn. Dec 1 st from neck edge on next row, then every other row 3 (4, 4, 5) times more—10 (11, 12, 12) sts. Work even until piece measures same length as back. Fasten off.

Right neck shaping

Next row (RS) Sk 2 center sts, join yarn with an hdc in next st, work to end—14 (16, 17, 18) sts. Ch 2, turn. Cont to work as for left neck, reversing shaping.

SLEEVES

Ch 22 (24, 27, 29).

Row 1 (WS) Hdc in 3rd ch from hook and in each ch across—20 (22, 25, 27) sts. Ch 2, turn.

Row 2 Hdc in each st across. Ch 2, turn. Rep row 2 for pat st and work even until piece measures 1 (1, 2, 2)"/2.5 (2.5, 5, 5)cm from beg. Inc 1 st each side every other row 3 times—26 (28, 31, 33) sts. Work even until piece measures 4 (5, 6, 7)"/10 (12.7, 15, 17.5)cm from beg. Fasten off.

COLLAR

(make 2 pieces)

Ch 15 (17, 19, 21).

Row 1 (WS) Sc in 2nd ch from hook and in each ch across—14 (16, 18, 20) sts. Ch 2, turn.

Row 2 Hdc in each st across. Ch 2, turn. Rep row 2 for pat st and inc 1 st each side every row 2 (3, 3, 4) times—18 (22, 24, 28) sts. Ch 3, turn.

Edging

Next row *Sk next st, work (dc, tr, dc) in next st, sk next st, sc in next st; rep from * to end of row, then cont along side edge (front edge of collar) to row 1. Fasten off.

FINISHING

Sew shoulder seams. Place markers 4½ (5, 5½, 6)"/11.5 (12.5, 14, 15)cm down from shoulder seams on front and back. Sew sleeves to armholes between markers. Sew side and sleeve seams. Sew on collar pieces.

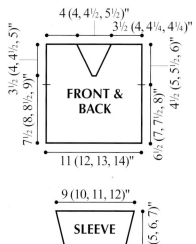

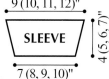

A confection-sweet poncho makes a sensible summertime cover-up when stitched with two strands of mohair/silk yarn held together. The decorative floral embellishments are knit separately, then sewn in place.

flower power

Instructions are written for size 18 months–3 years.

FINISHED MEASUREMENTS
• Rectangle 10" x 20"/25.5 x 51cm

MATERIALS
• *2 .85oz/25g balls (each approx 225yd/206m) of Knit One, Crochet Too's* **Douceur et Soie** *(mohair/silk) each in #8243 soft sunrise (A) and #8248 velvet rose (B)*

• *Size I/9 (5.5mm) crochet hook (for poncho) or size to obtain gauge*
• *Size G/6 (4mm) crochet hook (for flowers) or size to obtain gauge*

GAUGES
• 12 sts and 8 rows to 4"/10cm over dc using size I/9 (5.5mm) hook and 2 strands of yarn held tog.
• One flower to 4¾"/12cm using size G/6 (4mm) hook and 2 strands of yarn held tog.
Take time to check gauges.

NOTE
Use 2 strands of yarn held tog throughout.

PONCHO

(make 2 pieces)

With larger hook and one strand each of A and B held tog, ch 33.

Row 1 Dc in 4th ch from hook and in each ch across—30 sts. Ch 3, turn.

Row 2 Dc in each st across. Ch 3, turn. Rep row 2 for pat st and work even until piece measures 20"/51cm from beg. Fasten off.

FLOWERS

(make 16)

With smaller hook and 2 strands of A, ch 5. Join ch with a sl st forming a ring.

Rnd 1 Ch 1, work 16 sc over ring. Join rnd with a sl st in ch-1.

Rnd 2 [Ch 4, sk next 2 sts, sl st in next st] 5 times, end ch 4, sk last 2 sts, sl st in first ch of ch-4—6 ch-4 lps.

Rnd 3 Ch 1 (counts as 1 sc), work (4 dc, 1 tr, 4 dc, sc) in first ch-4 sp, * work (sc, 4 dc, 1 tr, 4 dc, sc) in next ch-4 sp; rep from * around 5 times. Join rnd with a sl st in ch-1.

Rnd 4 [Ch 5, sl st between next 2 sc (between petals)] 5 times, end ch 5, sl st in first ch of beg ch-5—6 ch-5 lps. Fasten off.

Rnd 5 Join 2 strands of B with a sl st in any ch-5 lp, ch 1, *work (sc, 5 dc, 3 tr, 5dc, sc) in next ch-5 lp; rep from * around 6 times. Join rnd with a sl st in ch-1. Fasten off.

FINISHING

Sew bottom edge of one poncho piece to side edge of second piece, outer side edges even. Sew opposite ends in the same manner forming a "V."

Neck edging

From RS, with larger hook and A and B held tog, join yarn with a sl st in center back neck edge.

Rnd 1 Ch 1, making sure that work lies flat, sc around neck edge. Join rnd with a sl st in ch-1. Fasten off. Sew flowers onto poncho, as shown.

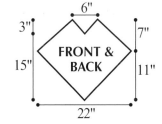

She'll be oh-so-pretty in pink wearing this pint-sized cardigan over a romper or dress. The unique tie-front stunner is crocheted in one piece and sports blanket-stitched accents along the edges.

party princess

SIZE

Instructions are written for size 6 months.

FINISHED MEASUREMENTS

- Chest (closed) 20"/51cm
- Length 9¹/₂"/24cm
- Upper arm 6"/15cm

MATERIALS

- 2 1³/₄oz/50g balls (each approx 151yd/138m) of Rowan Yarns/Westminster Fibers' **Kid Classic** (lambswool/mohair/nylon) in #819 pinched (MC)
- 1 ball in #833 cherish (CC)
- Size H/8 (5mm) crochet hook or size to obtain gauge
- Yarn needle

NOTE

The original colors used for this sweater are no longer available. The following substitutions are recommended:

- #844 frilly for #819 pinched (MC)
- #847 cherry red for #833 cherish (CC)

GAUGE

12 sts and 14 rows to 4"/10cm over pat st using size H/8 (5mm) hook.

Take time to check gauge.

NOTE

Sweater is made in one piece.

PATTERN STITCH

Row 1 *Sc in next dc, dc in next sc; rep from * to end. Ch 1, turn.

Rep row 1 for pat st.

BODY

Back

Beg at back bottom edge, with MC, ch 31.

Foundation row (RS) Sc in 2nd ch from hook, dc in next ch, *sc in next ch, dc in next ch; rep from * to end—30 sts. Ch 1, turn. Cont in pat st and work even until piece measures 6½"/16.5cm from beg, end with a WS row. Fasten off. Turn work.

Sleeves

Next row (RS) With MC, ch 18, cont in pat st across 30 back sts. Ch 19, turn.

Next row Sc in 2nd ch from hook, dc in next st, [sc in next ch, dc in next ch] 8 times, cont in pat st across 30 back sts, [sc in next ch, dc in next ch] 9 times—66 sts. Ch 1, turn. Work even until sleeve measures 3"/7.5cm from beg, end with a WS row.

Right neck shaping

Next row (RS) Work across first 30 sts. Ch 1, turn. **Note:** In order to maintain pat st when shaping, work as foll: when the last st worked is a sc, the first st on the next row will be a dc, so you must ch 3 (instead of ch 1) before turning. Dec 1 st at beg of next row, then at same edge every row once more—28 sts. Work even for 2 rows. Inc 1 st at neck edge on next row, then every row 4 times more—33 sts. Work even until sleeve measures 6"/15cm, end with a RS row.

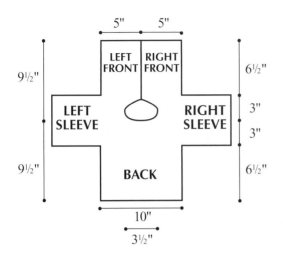

Right front

Next row (WS) Work across first 15 sts; leave rem 18 sts unworked for end of sleeve. Ch 3, turn. Cont in pat st for 6½"/16.5cm. Fasten off.

Left neck shaping

Next row (RS) Sk 6 center sts, join MC with a sc in next st, work to end. Ch 1, turn—30 sts. Cont to work as for right front, reversing shaping.

FINISHING

Sew side and sleeve seams

Embroidery

Use a single strand of CC in yarn needle. On RS, embroider a row of blanket stitches around fronts, neck and bottom edges. For sleeves, embroider blanket stitches on WS. Fold back cuffs; as shown.

Ties

(make 2)

With MC, make a ch that measures 10"/25.5cm-long.

Row 1 Sl st in 2nd ch from hook and in each ch across. Fasten off leaving a long tail for sewing. Sew ties at beg of neck shaping.

ynamic racer stripes and aqua-colored trim along the side seams offer plenty of spirit to this V-neck pullover. It's a cinch to stitch in half double crochet, and the relaxed fit takes this rough-and-tumble number day to night without missing a beat.

in the navy

SIZES

Instructions are written for size 6 months. Changes for sizes 12 months and 18 months are in parentheses.

FINISHED MEASUREMENTS

- Chest 22 (24, 26)"/56 (61, 66)cm
- Length 11 (12, 13)"/28 (30.5, 33)cm
- Upper arm 9 (10, 10)"/23 (25.5, 25.5)cm

MATERIALS

- 3 (4, 4) 1³/₄oz/50g balls (each approx 122yd/113m) of Rowan Yarns/Westminster Fibers' **Wool Cotton** (wool/cotton) in #909 french navy (MC) ③
- 1 (1, 2) ball in #901 citron (A)
- 1 ball in #949 aqua (B)
- Size G/6 (4mm) crochet hook or size to obtain gauge
- 2 bobbins
- Small safety pin

NOTE

One of the original colors used for this sweater is no longer available. The following substitution is recommended:

- #941 clear for #949 aqua (B)

GAUGE

15 sts and 12 rows to 4"/10cm over hdc using size G/6 (4mm) hook.

Take time to check gauge.

NOTES

1 See page 194 for how to work color changes.
2 Wind A onto 2 bobbins.

BACK

With MC, ch 36 (40, 44).

Row 1 (RS) Hdc in 3rd ch from hook and in each ch across—34 (38, 42) sts. Ch 2, turn.

Row 2 Hdc in each st across. Ch 2, turn. Rep row 2 for pat st and work even until piece measures 11 (12, 13)"/28 (30.5, 33)cm from beg. Fasten off.

FRONT

With A, ch 8, change to MC and ch 34 (38, 42), change to another bobbin of A and ch 10.

Row 1 (RS) With A, hdc in 3rd ch from hook and in next 7 ch, with MC, hdc in next 34 (38, 42) ch, with A, hdc in last 8 ch—50 (54, 58) sts. With A, ch 2, turn.

Row 2 With A, hdc in first 8 sts, with MC, hdc in next 34 (38, 42) sts, with A, hdc in last 8 sts. With A, ch 2, turn. Rep row 2 for pat st and color pat and work even until piece measures 6½ (7, 8)"/16.5 (17.5, 20.5)cm from beg, end with a WS row. Fasten off. Turn work.

Armhole shaping

Next row (RS) Sk first 8 sts, join MC with a hdc in next st, work across to within last 8 sts. With MC, ch 2, turn— 34 (38, 42) sts. Cont with MC only and work even until armhole measures 1½"/4cm, end with a WS row.

Left neck shaping

Next row (RS) Work across first 17 (19, 21) sts, ch 2, turn. Dec 1 st from neck edge every row 7 (8, 8) times— 10 (11, 13) sts. Work even until same length as back. Fasten off.

Right neck shaping

Next row (RS) Join MC with a hdc in next st, work to end. Cont to work as for left neck, reversing shaping.

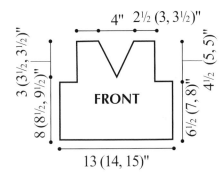

4" 2½ (3, 3½)"

3 (3½, 3½)"

8 (8½, 9½)"

FRONT

4½ (5, 5)"

6½ (7, 8)"

13 (14, 15)"

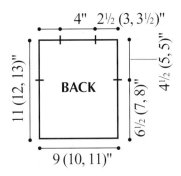

4" 2½ (3, 3½)"

11 (12, 13)"

BACK

4½ (5, 5)"

6½ (7, 8)"

9 (10, 11)"

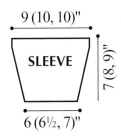

9 (10, 10)"

SLEEVE

7 (8, 9)"

6 (6½, 7)"

SLEEVES

With B, ch 24 (26, 28).

Row 1 (RS) Hdc in 3rd ch from hook and in each ch across—22 (24, 26) sts. Change to A, ch 2, turn.

Row 2 With A, hdc in first 4 sts, with MC, hdc in next 14 (16, 18) sts, with another bobbin of A, hdc last 4 sts. With A, ch 2, turn. Keeping 4 sts each side in A, inc 1 st each side of MC section on next row, then every 3rd row 5 (6, 5) times more—34 (38, 38) sts. Work even until piece measures 7 (8, 9)"/17.5 (20.5, 23)cm from beg, end with a WS row. Change to B, ch 2, turn.

Next row (RS) With A, hdc in first 4 sts, with B, hdc in next 26 (30, 30) sts, with A, hdc last 4 sts. Fasten off.

FINISHING

Sew shoulder, side and sleeve seams. Set in sleeves matching A stripes at underarms.

Neck edging

From RS, join MC with a sl st in left shoulder seam.

Rnd 1 Ch 1, making sure that work lies flat, sc to center of v shaping, sc in center, mark this st with the safety pin, cont to sc around remaining neck edge. Join rnd with a sl st in first st. Change to B.

Rnd 2 Ch 2, hdc in each st to within one st of mark st; remove safety pin. To dec across 3 sts, work as foll: [Yo, draw up a lp in next st] 3 times, yo and draw through all lps on hook. Cont to hdc in each st to end. Join rnd with a sl st in first st. Change to MC.

Rnd 3 Ch 1, working through back lps only, sc in each st around. Join rnd with a sl st in first st. Fasten off.

Traditional Peruvian folk art inspired the intricate design of this spirited poncho. Work the easy silhouette in one piece, create the design using half double crochet stitch and finish it off with fringes.

p o n c h o   p o w e r

SIZE

Instructions are written for size 12–18 months.

FINISHED MEASUREMENTS

Width 22"/56cm

Length 12"/30.5cm (not including fringe)

MATERIALS

ORIGINAL YARN

- 2 1¾oz /50g balls (each approx 103yd/95m) of Tahki Yarns/Tahki•Stacy Charles, Inc.'s **New Tweed** (wool/silk/viscose) each in #025 medium brown (A) and #05 dark brown (B) **4**
- 1 ball each in #1 beige (C) and #024 light brown (D)

SUBSTITUTE YARN

- 2 1¾oz/50g balls (each approx 118yd/108m) of Rowan Yarns/Westminster Fibers' **Summer Tweed** (silk/cotton) each in #530 toast (A) and #531 chocolate fudge (B) **4**
- 1 ball each in #508 oats (C) and #514 reed (D)
- Size H/8 (5mm) crochet hook or size to obtain gauge
- 1yd/1m of leather cord (optional)

GAUGE

12 sts and 10 rows to 4"/10cm over hdc using size H/8 (5mm) hook.

Take time to check gauge.

NOTES

1 See instructions on page 194 for how to work color changes for rows.

2 See instructions on page 194 for how to follow charts.

BACK

With A, ch 68.

Row 1 (WS) Hdc in 3rd ch from hook and in each ch across—66 sts. Ch 2, turn.

Row 2 Hdc in each st across. Ch 2, turn. Rep row 2 for pat st and work even for one more row.

Chart 1

Row 1 (RS) Beg with st 1 and work to st 6, then rep sts 1-6 10 times more. Cont to foll chart in this way to row 4, end with a WS row.

Chart 2

Row 1 (RS) Beg with st 1 and work to st 11, then rep sts 1-11 5 times more. Cont to foll chart in this way to row 21, end with a RS row.

Chart 3

Row 1 (WS) Beg with st 6 and work to st 1, then rep sts 6-1 10 times more. Cont to foll chart in this way to row 5; piece should measure 12"/30.5cm from beg. Fasten off.

FRONT

Work as for back until row 18 of chart 2 has been completed, end with a WS row; piece should measure 9"/23cm from beg.

Left neck shaping

Row 19 (RS) Work across first 33 sts. Ch 2, turn.

Dec 1 st at beg of next row, then at same edge every row 4 times. AT SAME TIME, when chart 2 has been completed, work chart 3. Work even on 28 sts to row 5 of chart 3. Fasten off.

Right neck shaping

Row 19 (RS) Join A with a sc in next st, work to end. Ch 2, turn. Cont to work as for left neck, reversing shaping.

FINISHING

Sew shoulder seams.

Neck edging

From RS, join A with a sc in right shoulder seam.

Rnd 1 Making sure that work lies flat, sc evenly around neck edge. Join rnd with a sl st in first st. Fasten off.

Fringe

For each fringe, cut 4 strands of B 9"/23cm long. Use hook to pull through and knot fringe. Knot 17 fringes across front and back bottom edges. Weave optional leather cord around neck edge, beg and ending at center front. Tie cord at neck, then knot ends.

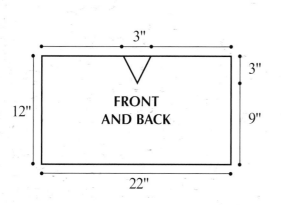

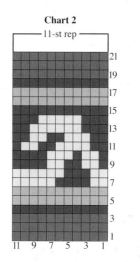

Chart 2
11-st rep

Chart 1
6-st rep

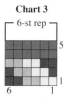

Chart 3
6-st rep

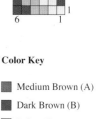

Color Key

- ■ Medium Brown (A)
- ■ Dark Brown (B)
- □ Beige (C)
- ■ Light Brown (D)

how your stripes and some fashion flair for any pint-sized outing. Complex-looking but easy to make, this sporty V-neck vest features basic shaping and contrast-colored edging. Stitched in a simple variation of single crochet, it works up in a jiffy with a big hook.

v e s t   f r i e n d

SIZES

Instructions are written for size 3–6 months.
Changes for sizes 9–12 months, 18–24 months and
3 years are in parentheses.

FINISHED MEASUREMENTS

- Chest 22 (24, 26, 28)"/56 (61, 66, 71)cm
- Length 11 (12, 13, 14)"/28 (30.5, 33, 35.5)cm

MATERIALS

ORIGINAL YARN

- 3 (4, 4, 5) 1¾oz/50g balls (each approx 70yd/64m) of
Classic Elite Yarns' **Follies** (rayon/alpaca/wool) in #3402
green (MC) **4**
- 1 ball in #3456 lavender (CC)

SUBSTITUTE YARN

- 4 (5, 5, 6) 1¾oz/50g balls (each approx 65yd/59m) of
Classic Elite Yarns' **Bazic Wool** (wool) in #2902 winter-
green (MC) **4**
- 1 ball in #2993 trojan blue (CC)
- Size H/8 (5mm) crochet hook or size to obtain gauge

GAUGE

14 sts and 14 rows to 4"/10cm over pat st using size
H/8 (5mm) hook.
Take time to check gauge.

PATTERN STITCH

(over an even number of sts)

Row 1 *Sc into front lp of next st, sc into back lp of next st; rep from * across. Ch 1, turn.

Rep row 1 for pat st.

BACK

With MC, ch 39 (43, 47, 51).

Foundation row Sc in 2nd ch from hook and in each ch across—38 (42, 46, 50) sts. Ch 1, turn. Cont in pat st and work even until piece measures 7 (7½, 8, 8½)"/17.5 (19, 20.5, 21.5)cm from beg. Do not ch, turn.

Armhole shaping

Sl st across first 4 (4, 5, 5) sts, ch 1, work in pat st across to within last 4 (4, 5, 5) sts, ch 1, turn—30 (34, 36, 40) sts. Work even until piece measures 11 (12, 13, 14)"/28 (30.5, 33, 35.5)cm from beg. Fasten off.

FRONT

Work as for back until piece measures 7½ (8, 8½, 9)"/19 (20.5, 21.5, 23)cm from beg. Ch 1, turn.

Left neck shaping

Next row Work across first 14 (16, 17, 19) sts. Ch 1, turn. Keeping to pat st, dec 1 st from neck edge every row twice, every other row 3 (4, 4, 5) times—9 (10, 11, 12) sts. Work even until same length as back. Fasten off.

Right neck shaping

Next row Sk 2 center sts, join yarn with a sc in next st, work to end. Cont to work as for left neck, reversing shaping.

FINISHING

Sew shoulder and side seams.

Neck edging

From RS, join CC with a sl st in left shoulder seam, ch 1. Making sure that work lies flat, sc around neck edge, dec 1 st over center 2 sts. Join rnd with a sl st in ch-1. Fasten off.

Armhole Edging

From RS, join CC with a sl st in underarm seam, ch 1. Making sure that work lies flat, sc around armhole edge. Join rnd with a sl st in ch-1. Fasten off.

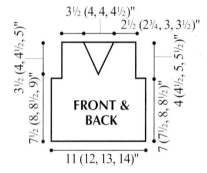

3½ (4, 4½)"

2½ (2¾, 3, 3½)"

3½ (4, 4½, 5)"

7½ (8, 8½, 9)"

FRONT & BACK

7 (7½, 8, 8½)"

4 (4½, 5, 5½)"

11 (12, 13, 14)"

The classic argyle vest is thoroughly updated in saturated hues. A variety of colored diamonds decorate the front body, while wraparound stripes provide contrast. The boxy silhouette offers all-day comfort.

versatile vest

SIZES

SIZES

Instructions are written for size 3–6 months.
Changes for sizes 9–12 months, 18–24 months and
3 years are in parentheses.

FINISHED MEASUREMENTS

- Chest 22 (24, 26, 28)"/56 (61, 66, 71)cm
- Length 12 (13, 14, 15)"/30.5 (33, 35.5, 38)cm

MATERIALS

ORIGINAL YARN

- 2 1¾oz/50g balls (each approx 138yd/126m) of
Classic Elite Yarns' **Waterspun** (wool) in #5035 lime
green (A) **4**
- 1 ball each in #5049 blue (B), #5050 olive green
(C), #5046 teal blue (D), #5027 red purple (E) and
#5068 orange (F)

SUBSTITUTE YARN

- 3 1¾oz/50g balls (each approx 110yd/100m) of
Classic Elite Yarns' **Renaissance** (wool) in #7135
celery (A) **4**
- 1 ball each in #7104 lapis (B), #7181 green grape
(C), #7146 alpine spruce (D), #7127 chianti (E) and
#7178 tiled roof (F)
- Size H/8 (5mm) crochet hook or size to obtain
gauge
- 9 bobbins

GAUGE

16 sts and 16 rows to 4"/10cm over pat st using size
H/8 (5mm) hook.
Take time to check gauge.

NOTES

1 See page 195 for how to work color changes for
argyle patterns.
2 Wind A onto 5 bobbins and B, C, D and E onto
separate bobbins.
3 See page 194 for how to work color changes for
rows.
4 See page 196 for how to embroider chain stitch.

PATTERN STITCH

Row 1 Sc in back lp of each st across. Ch 1, turn.
Rep row 1 for pat st.

STRIPE PATTERN

Working in pat st, work 1 row each B, C, D, E, F and A.
Rep these 6 rows for stripe pat.

BACK

With A, ch 53 (57, 65, 69).

Foundation row Sc in 2nd ch from hook and in each ch
across—52 (56, 64, 68) sts. Join B, ch 1, turn. Cont in
pat st and stripe pat and work even until piece measures
7½ (8, 8½, 9)"/19 (20, 21.5, 23)cm from beg.
Fasten off. Turn work.

Armhole shaping

Next row Keeping to stripe pat, sk first 8 (8, 12, 12) sts,
join next color with a sc in next st, work across to within last 8 (8, 12, 12) sts. Join next color, ch 1, turn—36
(40, 40, 44) sts. Work even until piece measures 12 (13,
14,15)"/30.5 (33, 35,5, 38)cm from beg. Fasten off.

FRONT

With A, ch 37 (41, 41, 45).

Foundation row Sc in 2nd ch from hook and in each ch
across—36 (40, 40, 44) sts. Ch 1, turn. Cont in pat st.

Beg chart

Row 5 (5, 3, 1) Beg with st 5 (3, 3, 1) and work to st
40 (42, 42, 44). Cont to foll chart in this way until row 42
is completed.

Left neck shaping

Row 43 (RS) Work across first 17 (19, 19, 21) sts, ch 1
turn. Dec 1 st from neck edge every row 4 times, every
other row 2 (3, 4, 5) times—11 (12, 11, 12) sts. Work
even until row 56 (58, 58, 60) is completed. Fasten off.

Right neck shaping

Row 43 (RS) Keeping to chart pat, sk 2 center sts, join
yarn with a sc in next st, work to end. Cont to work as
for left neck, reversing shaping.

FINISHING

Embroidery

Referring to chart, use F to embroider chain-stitch
diagonal lines. Sew shoulder and side seams.

Neck edging

From RS, join E with a sl st in left shoulder seam.

Rnd 1 Ch 1, making sure that work lies flat, sc around
neck edge. Join rnd with a sl st in ch-1. Fasten off. Rep
edging around each armhole and bottom edge.

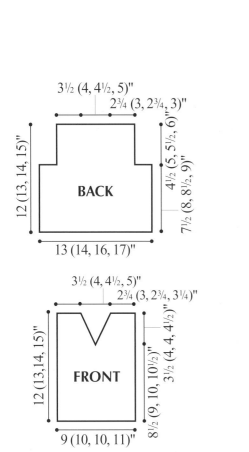

Color Key

- ☐ Lime (A)
- ▦ Blue (B)
- ▩ Olive (C)
- ■ Teal blue (D)
- ■ Red purple (E)
- ⦂ Orange (F) chain st

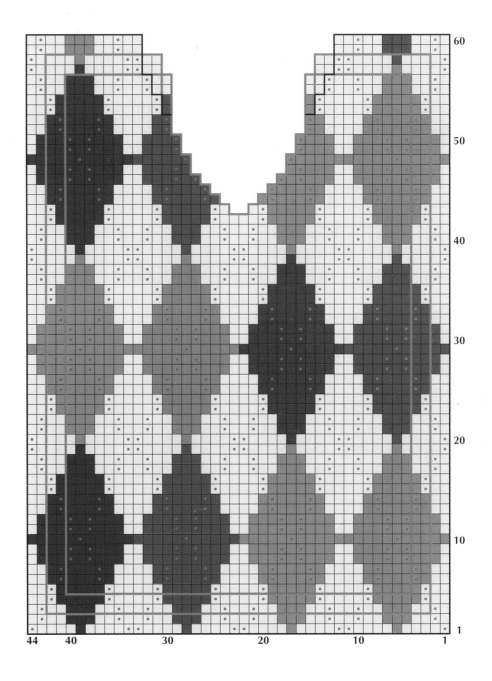

Yeah, baby! Go retro with this tie-front, fur-collared vest that looks great whether paired with a tiny A-line skirt or bell-bottom jeans. Featuring a simple repeat of stripes and textured stitches, this vintage-inspired number is as groovy to wear as it is to crochet.

hippie chic

Instructions are written for size 6–12 months. Changes for size 18 months–3 years are in parentheses.

FINISHED MEASUREMENTS

• Chest (closed) 25 (29)"/63.5 (73.5)cm

• Length 13½ (16)"/34 (40.5)cm

MATERIALS

ORIGINAL YARN

• 2 1¾oz/50g balls (each approx 128yd/117m) of Patons' **Country Garden DK** (wool) in #51 chocolate (A) **3**

• 1 ball each in #77 natural (B), #25 beetroot (C) and #28 wild violet (D)

• 1 3½oz/100g ball (approx 150yd/137m) of Friends Yarn's **Mustachio** (acrylic) in chocolate (E) **6**

SUBSTITUTE YARN

• 3 1¾oz/50g balls (each approx 105yd/96m) of Cleckheaton/Plymouth Yarn's **Country 8 Ply** (wool) in #2271 chocolate (A) **3**

• 2 balls each in #50 cream (B), #2160 raspberry (C) and #2246 lilac (D)

• 3 1¾oz/50g balls (approx 60yd/54m) of Lion Brand Yarn's **Fun Fur** (polyester) in #126 chocolate (E) **5**

• Size G/6 and I/9 (4 and 5.5mm) crochet hooks or sizes to obtain gauges

GAUGES

• 18 sts and 16 rows to 4"/10cm over hdc using size G/6 (4mm) hook and A.

• 11 sts and 10 rows to 4"/10cm over sc using size I/9 (5.5mm) hook and E.

Take time to check gauges.

NOTES

1 See page 194 for how to make color changes.

2 It is sometimes difficult to see the sts when working with furry yarn. For best results, count sts as you work across each row to make sure you do not skip or miss a st.

PATTERN STITCH

Row 1 (WS) Sc in first st, sk next st, *work 3 dc in next st (shell made), sk next st, sc in next st, sk next st; rep from *, end work 3 dc in next st (shell), sk next st, sc in last st. Join C, ch 3, turn.

Row 2 Work 2 dc in first sc (half shell made), sc in 3rd dc of next shell,* work 3 dc in next sc, sc in 3rd dc of next shell; rep from *, end work 2 dc in last sc. Join D, ch 1, turn.

Row 3 Sc in first 2 sts, *in next st work [yo, draw up a lp, yo, draw through 2 lps on hook] 3 times, yo and draw through all 4 lps on hook (bobble made), sc in next 3 sts; rep from *, end bobble in next st, sc in last 2 sts. Join A, ch 2, turn.

Rows 4 and 5 Hdc in each st across. After row 5 is completed, join B, ch 3, turn.

Row 6 Dc in first st, *dc between next 2 sts of row below, dc in next st; rep from * to end. Join C, ch 1, turn.

Row 7 Rep row 1. Join D, ch 3, turn.

Row 8 Rep row 2. Join A, ch 1, turn.

Work rows 1–8 for pat st.

STRIPE PATTERN 1

Row 1 Sc in each st across. Ch 2, turn.

Row 2 Hdc in each st across. Join B, ch 3, turn.

Row 3 Dc in first st, *dc between next 2 sts of row below, dc in next st; rep from * to end. Join C, ch 1, turn.

Row 4 Rep row 1. Join D, ch 1, turn.

Row 5 Rep row 1. Join C, ch 1, turn.

Row 6 Rep row 1. Join B, ch 3, turn.

Row 7 Dc in each st across. Join A, ch 2, turn.

Row 8 Rep row 2. Ch 1, turn.

Rows 9 and 10 Rep row 1. After row 10 is completed, join B, ch 1, turn.

Work rows 1–10 for stripe pat 1.

STRIPE PATTERN 2

Row 1 Sc in each st across. Ch 2, turn.

Rows 2–4 Hdc in each st across. After row 4 is completed, join B, ch 3, turn.

Row 5 Dc in first st, *dc between next 2 sts of row below, dc in next st; rep from * to end. Join C, ch 1, turn.

Row 6 Rep row 1. Join D, ch 1, turn.

Row 7 Rep row 1. Join C, ch 1, turn.

Row 8 Rep row 1. Join B, ch 3, turn.

Row 9 Dc in each st across. Join A, ch 2, turn.

Rows 10–12 Rep row 2. After row 12 is completed, ch 1, turn.

Rows 13 and 14 Rep row 1. After row 14 is completed, join B, ch 1, turn.

Work rows 1–14 for stripe pat 2.

BACK

With smaller hook and A, ch 55 (67). **Foundation row (RS)** Hdc in 3rd ch from hook and in each ch across—53 (65) sts. Join B, ch 1, turn. Work 8 rows of pat st, 10 (14) rows of stripe pat 1 (2), then 8 rows of pat st. Piece should measure 8½ (10)"/21.5 (25.5)cm from beg. Fasten off. Turn work.

Armhole shaping

Next row (WS) Sk first 4 sts, join A with a sc in next st, work row 1 of stripe pat 1 (2) across to within last 4 sts. Ch 2, turn—45 (57) sts. Work rem 9 (13) rows of stripe pat 1 (2), then work pat st until piece measures 13½ (16)"/34 (40.5)cm from beg. Fasten off.

LEFT FRONT

With smaller hook and A, ch 31 (35). **Foundation row (RS)** Hdc in 3rd ch from hook and in each ch across—29 (33) sts. Join B, ch 1, turn. Work 8 rows of pat st, 10 (14) rows of stripe pat 1 (2), then 8 rows of pat st.

Armhole shaping

Next row (WS) Working in stripe pat 1 (2), then pat st, work across to within last 4 sts. Ch 2, turn—25 (29) sts.

Neck shaping

Next row (RS) Work across, dec 1 st over last 2 sts. Cont to dec 1 st from (neck) edge every row 6 times more, every other row 5 times—13 (17) sts. Work even until piece measures same length as back. Fasten off.

RIGHT FRONT

Work as for left front to armhole shaping, then work 1 row of stripe pat 1 (2). Keeping to stripe pat and pat st, cont to work as for left front, reversing shaping.

COLLAR

With larger hook and E, ch 43 (53). **Foundation row** Sc in 2nd ch from hook and in each ch across—42 (52) sts. Ch 1, turn. Cont in sc.

Row 1 Dec 1 st over first 2 sts, sc in next 13 (16) sts, work 2 sc in next st, sc in next 10 (14) sts, work 2 sc in next st, sc in next 13 (16) sts, dec 1 st over last 2 sts—42 (52) sts. Ch 1, turn.

Row 2 Dec 1 st over first 2 sts, sc in next 12 (15) sts, [work 2 sc in next st] twice, sc in next 10 (14) sts, [work 2 sc in next st] twice, sc in next 12 (15) sts, dec 1 st over last 2 sts—44 (54) sts. Ch 1, turn.

Row 3 [Dec 1 st over 2 sts] twice, sc in next 11 (14) sts, [work 2 sc in next st] twice, sc in next 10 (14) sts, [work 2 sc in next st] twice, sc in next 11 (14) sts, [dec 1 st over next 2 sts] twice—44 (54) sts. Ch 1, turn.

Row 4 [Dec 1 st over 2 sts] twice, sc in next 36 (46) sts, [dec 1 st over next 2 sts] twice—40 (50) sts. Ch 1, turn.

Rows 5 and 6 Dec 1 st over first 2 sts, sc in next 12 (15) sts, work 2 sc in next st, sc in next 10 (14) sts, work 2 sc in next st, sc in next 12 (15) sts, dec 1 st over last 2 sts—40 (50) sts. Ch 1, turn.

Row 7 [Dec 1 st over 2 sts] twice, sc in next 32 (42) sts, [dec 1 st over next 2 sts] twice—36 (46) sts. Ch 1, turn.

Rows 8 and 9 Sc in each st across. Ch 1, turn. After row 9 is completed, fasten off.

FINISHING

Sew shoulder and side seams.

Edging

From RS with smaller hook, join A with a sl st in left side seam. **Rnd 1** Ch 1, making sure that work lies flat, sc around entire edge, working 3 sc in each corner. Join rnd with a sl st in ch-1. Fasten off.

Armhole edging

From RS with smaller hook, join A with a sl st in side seam. **Rnd 1** Ch 1, making sure that work lies flat, sc around armhole edge. Join rnd with a sl st in ch-1. Fasten off. Sew on collar.

Ties

(make 4)

With smaller hook and A, ch 36. Fasten off. Sew a pair of ties at beg of collar and the other pair 2 (2½)"/5 (6)cm below.

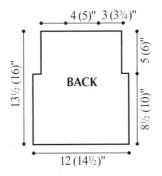

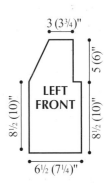

fur real

No need to sacrifice style for comfort—the sumptuous faux-fur yarn does all the work in this plush sensation. Simply stitch it up in single crochet and embellish the cardigan with whimsical buttons.

SIZES

Instructions are written for size 3–6 months. Changes for sizes 9–12 months, 18–24 months and 3 years are in parentheses.

FINISHED MEASUREMENTS

- Chest (buttoned) 22 (24, 26, 28)"/56 (61, 66, 71)cm
- Length 11 (12, 13, 14)"/28 (30.5, 33, 35.5)cm
- Upper arm 10 (11, 11½, 12)"/25.5 (28, 29, 30.5)cm

MATERIALS

ORIGINAL YARN

- 4 (5, 5, 6) 3½oz/100g balls (each approx 150yd/137m) of Friends Yarn's **Mustachio** (acrylic) in #03 burgundy **6**

SUBSTITUTE YARN

- 9 (11, 11, 13) 1¾oz/50g balls (each approx 72yd/66m) of Moda Dea/Coats & Clark's **Prima** (nylon/polyester) in #3377 burgundy **5**
- Size I/9 (5.5mm) crochet hook or size to obtain gauge
- 3 ⅞"/22mm buttons
- 1 set of markers

GAUGE

11 sts and 10 rows to 4"/10cm over sc using size I/9 (5.5mm) hook.
Take time to check gauge.

NOTE

It is sometimes difficult to see the sts when working with furry yarn. For best results, count sts as you work across each row to make sure you do not skip or miss a st.

BACK

Ch 31 (35, 37, 39).

Row 1 Sc in 2nd ch from hook and in each ch across—30 (34, 36, 38) sts. Ch 1, turn.

Row 2 Sc in each st across. Ch 1, turn. Rep row 2 for pat st and work even until piece measures 11 (12, 13, 14)"/28 (30.5, 33, 35.5)cm from beg. Fasten off.

LEFT FRONT

Ch 17 (19, 20, 22).

Row 1 Sc in 2nd ch from hook and in each ch across—16 (18, 19, 21) sts. Ch 1, turn. Work even in sc until piece measures 7 (7½, 8, 8½)"/17.5 (19, 20.5, 21.5)cm from beg.

Neck shaping

Next row (RS) Work across to last 2 sts, dec 1 st over last 2 sts. Cont to dec 1 st from same edge every row 4 (5, 6, 7) times more—11 (12, 12, 13) sts. Work even until piece measures same length as back. Fasten off.

RIGHT FRONT

Work as for left front reversing neck shaping.

SLEEVES

Ch 17 (19, 21, 23).

Row 1 Sc in 2nd ch from hook and in each ch across—16 (18, 20, 22) sts. Ch 1, turn. Work in sc and inc 1 st each side every other row 6 times—28 (30, 32, 34) sts.

BACK

3 (3½, 4½, 4½)"
4 (4¼, 4¼, 4¾)"
11 (12, 13, 14)"
11 (12, 13, 14)"
6 (6½, 7¼, 8)"
5 (5½, 5¾, 6)"

LEFT FRONT

4 (4¼, 4¼, 4¾)"
7 (7½, 8, 8½)"
6 (6½, 7, 7½)"
6 (6½, 7¼, 8)"
5 (5½, 5¾, 6)"

SLEEVE

10 (11, 11½, 12)"
7 (8, 9, 10)"
6 (6½, 7, 8)"

Work even until piece measures 7 (8, 9, 10)"/17.5 (20, 23, 25.5)cm from beg. Fasten off.

FINISHING

Sew shoulder seams. Place markers 5 (5½, 5¾, 6)"/12.5 (14, 14.5, 15)cm down from shoulder seams on fronts and back. Sew sleeves to armholes between markers. Sew side and sleeve seams.

Button loops

(make 3)

Ch 8. Fasten off leaving a long tail for sewing. Fold ch in half to make loop. On right front, sew first loop at beg of neck shaping and the others spaced 2"/5cm apart. Sew on buttons.

In a kaleidoscope of jewel-tone colors, this delightful hooded coat is a dream to wear for fashion-minded tots! Vibrant granny squares are crocheted together; the coat is then completed with a simple edging.

spice girl

SIZES

Instructions are written for size 6–12 months. Changes for sizes 24 months–3 years are in parentheses.

FINISHED MEASUREMENTS

- Chest (buttoned) 24 (30)"/61 (76)cm
- Length 16 (20)"/40.5 (51)cm
- Upper arm 10 (12½)"/25.5 (31.5)cm

MATERIALS

- *6 (8) 1¾oz/50g balls (each approx 110yd/100m) of Noro/KFI's **Kureyon** (wool) in #102 fuchsia brights*

- *Size G/6 (4mm) crochet hook (for size 6–12 months) or size to obtain gauge*
- *Size I/9 (5.5mm) crochet hook (for size 24 months–3 years) or size to obtain gauge*
- *3 ⅞"/22mm buttons*
- *1 set of markers*

GAUGES

- One square to 2"/5cm using size G/6 (4mm) hook.
- One square to 2½"/6cm using size I/9 (5.5mm) hook.

Take time to check gauge.

NOTE

See page 196 for granny square basics.

GRANNY SQUARES

(make 158)

Work as for solid color basic granny square working rnds 1 and 2.

HALF-SQUARES

(make 2)

Work as for basic granny half-square.

QUARTER-SQUARES

(make 8)

Work as for basic granny quarter-square.

FINISHING

Refer to placement diagrams. Sew squares tog to form back and hood. Sew squares and half-squares tog to form fronts. Sew squares and quarter-squares tog to form sleeves. Sew shoulder seams. Place markers 5 (6¼)"/12.5 (16)cm down from shoulder seams on fronts and back. Sew sleeves to armholes between markers. Sew side and sleeve seams. Fold hood in half and sew back seam. Sew hood to neck edge, beg and ending above half-square at each neck edge and easing in fullness along neck edge.

Edging

From RS, join yarn with a sl st in left side seam, ch 1. Making sure that work lies flat, sc around entire edge working 3 sc in each corner. Join rnd with a sl st in ch-1. Fasten off.

Button loops

(make 3)

Ch 8. Fasten off leaving a long tail for sewing. Fold ch in half to make loop. On right front, sew first loop at base of half-square at neck and the others spaced 2 (2½)"/5 (6)cm apart. Sew on buttons.

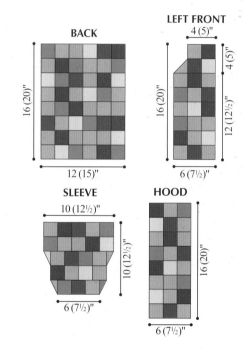

BACK

16 (20)"

12 (15)"

LEFT FRONT

4 (5)"

4 (5)"

16 (20)"

12 (12½)"

6 (7½)"

SLEEVE

10 (12½)"

10 (12½)"

6 (7½)"

HOOD

16 (20)"

6 (7½)"

When temperatures drop, carefree accessories zap the chills away! Embellished with fringe and pompoms, this captivating set of stylish winter warmers will be a favorite all season long.

square toppers

Instructions are written for size 6–12 months. Changes for sizes 18 months–3 years are in parentheses.

FINISHED MEASUREMENTS

Hat

- Circumference 17 (19)"/43 (48)cm

Scarf

- 5" x 30"/12.5 x 76cm (not including fringe)

MATERIALS

ORIGINAL YARN

- 2 (3) 1¾oz/50g balls (each approx 131yd/120m) of Knit One, Crochet Too's **Creme Brulee** (wool) in #235 deep plum (E) ③
- 1 ball each in #513 key lime (A), #527 kiwi (B), #620 powder blue (C) and #789 violet (D)

SUBSTITUTE YARN

- 3 (4) 1¾oz/50g balls (each approx 105yd/96m) of Cleckheaton/Plymouth Yarn's **Country 8 Ply** (wool) in #2160 raspberry (E) ③
- 1 ball each in #2234 pale yellow (A), #2250 lime (B), #2250 blue (c) and #2246 lilac (D)
- Size G/6 (4mm) crochet hook or size to obtain gauges

GAUGES

- 16 sts and 12 rnds to 4"/10cm over hdc using size G/6 (4mm) hook.
- One square to 5"/12.5cm using size G/6 (4mm) hook.

Take time to check gauges.

NOTES

1 See page 194 for how to make color changes.

2 See page 196 for granny square basics.

Work 1 row each C, D, E, A and B.

Rep these 5 rows for stripe pat.

HAT

Brim

With A, ch 70 (78).

Row 1 Hdc in 3rd ch from hook and in each ch across—68 (76) sts. Join B, ch 2, turn.

Row 2 Hdc in each st across. Join C, ch 2, turn. Cont in hdc and stripe pat, and work even until piece measures 4 (5)"/10 (12.5)cm from beg.

For size 6-12 months only

Next row *Hdc in next 10 sts, work 2 hdc in next st; rep from * across, end hdc in last 2 sts—74 sts.

Next row *Hdc in next 11 sts, work 2 hdc in next st; rep from * across, end hdc in last 2 sts—80 sts. Fasten off.

For size 18 months-3 years only

Next row *Hdc in next 18 sts, work 2 hdc in next st; rep from * across—80 sts. Fasten off.

For both sizes

Work even until piece measures 5 (6)"/12.5 (15)cm frm beg. Fasten off.

GRANNY SQUARES

(make 4)

Work as for multi-color basic granny square working rnd 1 with A, rnd 2 with B, rnd 3 with C, rnd 4 with D and rnd 5 with E.

FINISHING

Sew squares tog forming a strip. Sew brim to strip. Sew side seam. Working from the side in, sew top edges of squares tog halfway; they will all meet in the center forming 4 points.

Pompoms

(make 4)

Using all colors, make a 2¼"/6cm in diameter pompom (see pompom instructions). Sew a pompom to each point, as shown. Fold back brim.

SCARF

Make 6 granny squares as for hat.

FINISHING

Sew squares tog forming a strip.

Fringe

For each fringe, cut each color 6"/15cm long. Use hook to pull through and knot fringe. At each end of scarf, knot 6 fringe across.

A chic fur-trimmed coat offers no-fuss style and flair to any little girl's wardrobe. Defined by modest A-line shaping, an allover half double crochet pattern and sumptuous fur collar and cuffs, it's truly a modern classic.

raspberry rhapsody

SIZES

Instructions are written for size 12 months. Changes for sizes 24 months and 3 years are in parentheses.

FINISHED MEASUREMENTS

• Chest (buttoned) 24 (26, 28)"/61 (66, 71)cm

• Length 16 (19, 21)"/40.5 (48, 53)cm

• Upper arm 10 (12, 13)"/25.5 (30.5, 33)cm

MATERIALS

ORIGINAL YARN

• *3 (4, 5) 5oz/140g balls (each approx 260yd/238m) of TLC/Coats & Clark's **Heathers** (acrylic) in #5745 medium pink (MC)*

• *4 (5, 6) 3½oz/100g balls (each approx 150yd/137m) of Friends Yarn's **Mustachio** (acrylic) in off white (CC)*

SUBSTITUTE YARN

• *4 (6, 7) 3½oz/100g balls (each approx 190yd/174m) of Red Heart/Coats & Clark's **Classic** (acrylic) in #761 light berry (MC)*

• *2 (2, 3) 1¾oz/50g balls (each approx 60yd/54m) of Lion Brand Yarn's **Fun Fur** (polyester) in #98 ivory (CC)*

• *Size H/8 and I/9 (5 and 5.5mm) crochet hooks or sizes to obtain gauges*

• *4 ¾"/19mm buttons*

• *1 set of markers*

GAUGES

14 sts and 10 rows to 4"/10cm over pat st using size H/8 (5mm) hook and MC.

11 sts and 10 rows to 4"/10cm over sc using size I/9 (5.5mm) hook and CC.

Take time to check gauges.

NOTE

It is sometimes difficult to see the sts when working with furry yarn. For best results, count sts as you work across each row to make sure you do not skip or miss a st.

PATTERN STITCH

(over an even number of sts)

Row 1 *Hdc into front lp of next st, hdc into back lp of next st; rep from * across. Ch 2, turn.

Rep row 1 for pat st.

BACK

With smaller hook and MC, ch 57 (65, 71). **Foundation row** Sc in 2nd ch from hook and in each ch across—56 (64, 70) sts. Ch 2, turn. Cont in pat st and work even for 1"/2.5cm. Keeping to pat st, dec 1 st each side every 2nd row 3 (4, 4) times, every 4th row 4 (5, 6) times—42 (46, 50) sts. Work even until piece measures 11 (13, 14½)"/ 28 (33, 37)cm from beg. Do not ch, turn.

Armhole shaping

Next row Sl st across first 4 sts, ch 2, work across to within last 4 sts, ch 2, turn—34 (38, 42) sts. Work even until armhole measures 4½ (5½, 6)"/11.5 (14, 15)cm.

Right shoulder

Next row Work across first 10 (10, 12) sts. Ch 2, turn. Work even for 1 row. Fasten off.

Left shoulder

Next row Sk 14 (18, 18) center sts, join yarn with a hdc in next st, work to end. Work even for 1 more row. Fasten off.

LEFT FRONT

With smaller hook and MC, ch 29 (33, 37). **Foundation row** Sc in 2nd ch from hook and in each ch across—28 (32, 36) sts. Ch 2, turn. Cont in pat st and work even for 1"/2.5cm, end with a WS row. Keeping to pat st, dec 1 st at beg of next row, then at same edge every 2nd row 2 (3, 3) times more, every 4th row 4 (5, 6) times— 21 (23, 26) sts. Work even until piece measures 11 (13, 14½)"/28 (33, 37)cm from beg, end with a WS row. Do not ch, turn.

Armhole shaping

Next row (RS) Sl st across first 4 sts, ch 2, work to end—17 (19, 22) sts. Work even until armhole measures 3 (3½, 3½)"/7.5 (9, 9)cm from beg, end with a WS row.

Neck shaping

Next row (RS) Work across to within last 4 (4, 5) sts. Ch 2, turn. Dec 1 st from neck edge every row 3 (5, 5) times—10 (10, 12) sts. Work even until piece measures same length as back. Fasten off.

RIGHT FRONT

Work as for left front reversing shaping.

SLEEVES

With smaller hook and MC, ch 25 (27, 29). **Foundation row** Sc in 2nd ch from hook and in each ch across—24 (26, 28) sts. Ch 2, turn. Cont in pat st and work even for 1"/2.5cm. Keeping to pat st, inc 1 st each side every other row 3 (5, 6) times, every 4th row 3 times—36 (42, 46) sts. Work even until piece measures 9 (10, 11)"/23 (25.5, 28)cm from beg. Fasten off.

COLLAR

With larger hook and CC, ch 31 (39, 43). **Foundation row** Sc in 2nd ch from hook and in each ch across—30 (38, 42) sts. Ch 1, turn.

Row 1 Sc in first st, inc in next st, sc in next 2 sts, inc in next st, sc in next 5 (7, 9) sts, inc in next st, sc in next 8 (12, 12) sts, inc in next st, sc in next 5 (7, 9) sts, inc in next st, sc in next 2 sts, inc in next st, sc in last st—36 (44, 48) sts. Ch 1, turn.

Row 2 Sc in first st, inc in next st, sc in next 3 sts, inc in next st, sc in next 6 (8, 10) sts, inc in next st, sc in next 10 (14, 14) sts, inc in next st, sc in next 6 (8, 10) sts, inc in next st, sc in next 3 sts, inc in next st, sc in last st—42 (50, 54) sts. Ch 1, turn.

Row 3 Sc in first st, inc in next st, sc in next 4 sts, inc in next st, sc in next 7 (9, 11) sts, inc in next st, sc in next 12 (16, 16) sts, inc in next st, sc in next 7 (9, 11) sts, inc in next st, sc in next 4 sts, inc in next st, sc in last st—48 (56, 60) sts. Ch 1, turn.

Row 4 Sc in first st, inc in next st, sc in next 5 sts, inc in next st, sc in next 8 (10, 12) sts, inc in next st, sc in next 14 (18, 18) sts, inc in next st, sc in next 8 (10, 12) sts, inc in next st, sc in next 5 sts, inc in next st, sc in last st—54 (62, 66) sts. Ch 1, turn.

Row 5 Sc in first st, inc in next st, sc in next 6 sts, inc in next st, sc in next 9 (11, 13) sts, inc in next st, sc in next 16 (20, 20) sts, inc in next st, sc in next 9 (11, 13) sts, inc in next st, sc in next 6 sts, inc in next st, sc in last st—60 (68, 72) sts. Ch 1, turn.

Row 6 Sc in first st, inc in next st, sc in next 7 sts, inc in next st, sc in next 10 (12, 14) sts, inc in next st, sc in next 18 (22, 22) sts, inc in next st, sc in next 10 (12, 14) sts, inc in next st, sc in next 7 sts, inc in next st, sc in last st—66 (74, 78) sts. Ch 1, turn. Work 1 row even. Fasten off.

CUFFS

With larger hook and CC, ch 21 (23, 25). **Foundation row** Sc in 2nd ch from hook and in each ch across—20 (22, 24) sts. Ch 1, turn. Work even in sc for 2 rows. **Inc row** Sc in first st, inc in next st, sc in each st to within last 2 sts, inc in next st, sc in last st—22 (24, 26) sts. Ch 1, turn. Work 1 row even. Ch 1, turn. Rep last 2 rows once more—24 (26, 28) sts. Fasten off.

FINISHING

Sew shoulder seams.

Button band

With RS facing, smaller hook and MC, work 1 row of sc evenly along left front edge. Ch 1, turn. Work 2 rows even. Fasten off. Place markers on band for 4 buttons, with the first 1"/2.5cm from neck edge and the others spaced 2"/5cm apart.

Buttonhole band

Work as for buttonband until 1 row has been completed.

Buttonhole row *Sc to marker, ch 2, sk next 2 sts; rep from * to end. Ch 1, turn. **Next row** Sc in each st and work 2 sc in each ch-2 sp across. Fasten off. Set in sleeves, sewing last 1"/2.5cm at top of sleeve to armhole sts. Sew side and sleeve seams. Sew on collar and cuffs. Sew on buttons.

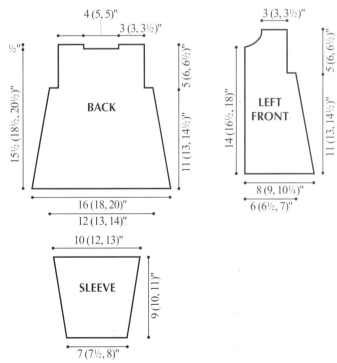

Two easy-stitch rectangles make up this chic argyle hat. Add a half double crochet stripe scarf with multicolored pompoms and he's off for a day of fun in the snow!

pompom panache

SIZES

Instructions are written for size 6–12 months. Changes for size 18 months–3 years are in parentheses.

FINISHED MEASUREMENTS

Hat

• Circumference 16 (19)"/40.5 (48)cm

Scarf

• 4" x 32" (4" x 36")/10 x 81 (10 x 91.5)cm

MATERIALS

ORIGINAL YARN

• 1 1¾oz/50g ball (each approx 138yd/ 126m) of Classic Elite Yarns' **Waterspun** (wool) in #5035 lime green (A), #5046 teal blue (B), #5027 red purple (C), #5068 orange (D), #5049 blue (F) and #5050 olive green (E) 🔢4

SUBSTITUTE YARN

• 2 1¾oz/50g balls (each approx 110yd/100m) of Classic Elite Yarns' **Renaissance** (wool) each in #7135 celery (A), #7146 alpine spruce (B), #7127 chianti (C), #7178 tiled roof (D), #7172 green pepper (E) and #7104 lapis (F) 🔢4

• Size H/8 (5mm) crochet hook or size to obtain gauges

• 5 bobbins

GAUGES

• 16 sts and 16 rows to 4"/10cm over pat st 1 using size H/8 (5mm) hook.

• 16 sts and 12 rows to 4"/10cm over pat st 2 using size H/8 (5mm) hook.

Take time to check gauges.

NOTES

1 See page 195 for how to work color changes for argyle patterns.

2 Wind A onto 3 bobbins, and B and C onto separate bobbins.

3 See page 194 for how to work color changes for rows.

4 See page 196 for how to embroider chain stitch.

PATTERN STITCH 1

Row 1 Sc in back lp of each st across. Ch 1, turn.
Rep row 1 for pat st 1.

PATTERN STITCH 2

Row 1 Hdc in back lp of each st across. Ch 2, turn.
Rep row 1 for pat st 2.

STRIPE PATTERN

Working in pat st 2, work 1 row each D, F, A, E, B and C.
Rep these 6 rows for stripe pat.

HAT

FRONT

With A, ch 33 (39).

Foundation row (RS) Sc in 2nd ch from hook and in
each ch across—32 (38) sts. Ch 1, turn. Cont in
pat st 1.

Beg chart

Row 3 (1) Beg with st 4 (1) and work to st 35 (38). Cont
to foll chart in this way until row 28 (30) is completed.
Fasten off.

BACK

With B, ch 33 (39).

Foundation row Sc in 2nd ch from hook and in each ch
across—32 (38) sts. Ch 1, turn. Cont in pat st 1 and
work even until piece measure same length as front.
Fasten off.

FINISHING

Embroidery

Referring to chart, use D to embroider chain-stitch
diagonal lines on front. Referring to same chart, use F to
embroider chain-stitch diagonal lines on back. Place
front and back tog, WS facing. With front facing you,
use D to sc pieces tog working 3 sc in each corner.
Fasten off.

Edging

From RS, join C with a sl st in side seam.

Rnd 1 Ch 1, sc in each st around—66 (78) sts. Join rnd
with a sl st in ch-1changing to D.

Rnd 2 Ch 1, sc in back lp of each st around. Join rnd
with a sl st in ch-1 changing to F.

Rnd 3 Rep rnd 2, changing to B.

Rnd 4 Rep rnd 2. Fasten off.

Pompoms

(make 2)

Using all colors, make a 2"/5cm in diameter pompom
(see pompom instructions). Sew a pompom to each
corner of hat.

SCARF

Beg at side edge with C, ch 130 (156).

Foundation row Hdc in 3rd ch from hook and in each ch across—128 (154) sts. Join D, ch 2, turn. Cont in pat st 2 and stripe pat and work even until piece measures 4"/10cm from beg. Fasten off.

FINISHING

Pompoms

(make 6)

Using all colors, make a 1½"/4cm in diameter pompom (see pompom instructions). Sew 3 pompoms across each end of scarf.

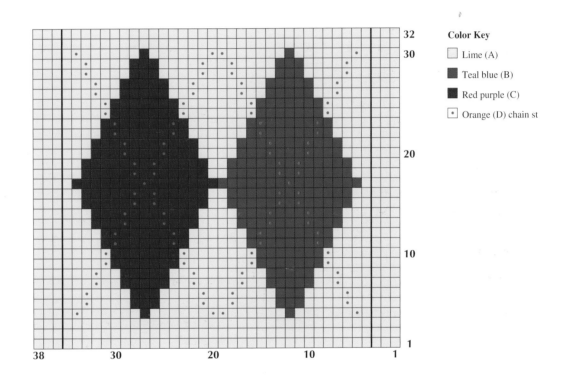

Color Key

☐ Lime (A)

■ Teal blue (B)

■ Red purple (C)

⊡ Orange (D) chain st

This vintage-inspired hat-and-vest set is nothing short of fabulous for color-craving tots. Whimsical bobble accents and a faux-fur trim jazz up the tie-front vest while an oh-so-cute granny-square hat with earflaps completes the look.

pastel parfait

SIZES

Instructions are written for size 6 months. Changes for sizes 12 months and 18 months are in parentheses.

FINISHED MEASUREMENTS

Vest

• Chest (closed) 20 (22, 24)"/51 (56, 61)cm

• Length 10 (11, 12)"/25.5 (28, 30.5)cm

Hat

• Circumference 15"/38cm

MATERIALS

ORIGINAL YARN

• 1 1³/₄oz/50g ball (each approx 152yd/139m) of Cleckheaton/Plymouth Yarns' **Angora Supreme** (lambswool/angora) each in #7 dark purple (A), #3 lavender (B), #5 turquoise (C), #6 dark pink (D) and #4 medium pink (E) 【4】

• 1 1³/₄oz/50g ball (approx 90yd/83m) of Berroco, Inc.'s **Plush** (nylon) in #1901 crema (F) 【5】

SUBSTITUTE YARN

• 3 1³/₄oz/50g balls (each approx 85yd/78m) of Debbie Bliss/KFI's **Cotton Angora** (cotton/angora) each in #13 maroon (A), #17 lavender (B), #26 light blue (C), #30 dusty rose (D) and #28 pink (E) 【4】

• 1 ball of Berroco, Inc.'s **Plush** in #1901 crema (F) (same as original)

• Size H/8 (5mm) crochet hook or size to obtain gauge

GAUGES

• 12 sts and 10 rows to 4"/10cm over hdc using size H/8 (5mm) hook.

• One granny square to 3³/₄"/9.5cm using size H/8 (5mm) hook.

Take time to check gauges.

NOTES

1 Body is worked in one piece to armhole, then both fronts and back are worked separately to shoulder.

2 See page 194 for how to work color changes for rows.

VEST

PATTERN STITCH

Row 1 (WS) Hdc in first 2 (3, 2) sts, *in next st work (yo, draw up a lp, yo, draw through 2 lps on hook) 3 times, yo and draw through all 4 lps on hook (bobble made), hdc in next 3 sts; rep from *, end bobble in next st, hdc in last 1 (2, 1) sts. Join C, ch 1, turn.

Row 2 Sc in each st across. Join D, ch 2, turn.

Rows 3 and 4 Hdc in each st across. Ch 2, turn. After row 4 is completed, join E, ch 3, turn.

Row 5 *Dc in next 2 sts, dc between next 2 sts of row below; rep from * to end. Join A, ch 2, turn.

Rows 6 and 7 Hdc in each st across. Ch 2, turn. After row 7 is completed, join B, ch 2, turn.

Rows 8 and 9 Hdc in each st across. Ch 2, turn. After row 9 is completed, join D, ch 2, turn.

Row 10 Hdc in each st across. Join E, ch 2, turn.

Row 11 Hdc in each st across. Join A, ch 2, turn.

Row 12 Hdc in each st across. Join B, ch 2, turn. Rep rows 1–12 for pat st.

BODY

With A, ch 62 (68, 74).

Foundation row (RS) Hdc in 3rd ch from hook and in each ch across—60 (66, 72) sts. Join B, ch 2, turn. Cont in pat st and work even until piece measures 6½ (7, 7½)"/16.5 (17.5, 19)cm from beg, end with a WS row.

Right front

Next row (RS) Work across first 12 (13, 14) sts. Keeping to pat st, ch and turn. Work even until armhole measures 1"/2.5cm, end with a WS row.

Neck shaping

Next row (RS) Dec 1 st at beg of row, then at same edge every row 5 (6, 7) times more—6 sts. Work even until armhole measures 3½ (4, 4½)"/9 (10, 11.5)cm. Fasten off.

Back

Next row (RS) Sk next 6 (7, 8) sts, join color in progress with a hdc in next st, then cont in pat st across next 23 (25, 27) sts. Keeping to pat st, ch and turn—24 (26, 28) sts. Work even until back measures same length as right front. Fasten off.

Left front

Next row (RS) Sk next 6 (7, 8) sts, join color in progress with a hdc in next st, then cont in pat st across last 11 (12, 13) sts. Keeping to pat st, ch and turn—12 (13, 14) sts. Cont to work same as right front, reversing neck shaping.

FINISHING

From RS, sc shoulders tog using E.

Trim

Trim is worked in chain st. Take care to maintain st and row gauge as you work. Position vest so bottom edge of left front is at top and RS is facing you. Make a slip knot in end of F. Insert hook between first and 2nd sts on bottom edge. On WS, place slip knot on hook and draw up to RS. Insert hook between 2nd and 3rd sts and draw up a lp, then draw through lp on hook—first chain st made. Insert hook between 3rd and 4th sts and draw up a lp, then draw through lp on hook—2nd chain st made. Working from right to left, cont in chain st around entire outer edge. Fasten off.

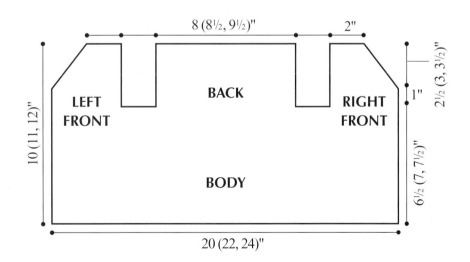

Armhole trim

Beg at side seam, work chain st same as above.

Ties

(make 4)

With D, make a ch that measures 6"/15cm-long. Fasten off leaving a long tail for sewing. Sew first pair of ties at beg of neck shaping and 2nd pair 2½"/6.5cm below.

HAT

BASIC GRANNY SQUARE

Ch 4. Join ch with a sl st forming a ring.

Rnd 1 (RS) Ch 3 (always counts as 1 dc), work 2 dc over ring, ch 2, *work 3 dc over ring, ch 2; rep from * 3 times. Join rnd with a sl st in 3rd ch of ch-3. Fasten off. From WS, join next color with a sl st in any ch-2 sp.

Rnd 2 Ch 3, work 2 dc in same ch-2 sp, ch 1, *work (3 dc, ch 2, 3 dc) in next ch-2 sp, ch 1; rep from * 3 times, end with 3 dc in beg ch-2 sp, ch 2. Join rnd with a sl st in 3rd ch of ch-3. Fasten off. From RS, join next color with a sl st in any ch-2 sp.

Rnd 3 Ch 3, work 2 dc in same ch-2 sp, ch 1, *work 3 dc in next ch-1 sp, ch 1, work (3 dc, ch 2, 3 dc) in next ch-2 sp, ch 1; rep from * 3 times, end with 3 dc in next ch-1 sp, ch 1, 3 dc in beg ch-2 sp, ch 2. Join rnd with a sl st in 3rd ch of ch-3. Fasten off. From WS, join next color with a sl st in any ch-2 sp.

Rnd 4 Ch 1 (counts as 1 sc), work 2 sc in same ch-2 sp, cont to sc in each st around, working 3 sc in each corner. Join rnd with a sl st in ch-1. Fasten off leaving a long tail for sewing.

BRIM

Make 4 basic granny squares in the following color combinations:

Square 1 Rnd 1 C, rnd 2 B, rnd 3 D and rnd 4 A.

Square 2 Rnd 1 D, rnd 2 B, rnd 3 A and rnd 4 E.

Square 3 Rnd 1 B, rnd 2 E, rnd 3 D and rnd 4 A.

Square 4 Rnd 1 E, rnd 2 A, rnd 3 B and rnd 4 D.

Working through back lps, sew squares tog forming a ring.

Top edging

From RS, join D with a sc in any st.

Rnd 1 Sc in each st around. Join rnd with a sl st in first st. Fasten off.

Bottom edging

From RS, join E with a sc in any st.

Rnd 1 Sc in each st around. Join rnd with a sl st in first st. Fasten off.

CROWN

With E, ch 4. Join ch with a sl st forming a ring.

Rnd 1 (RS) Ch 3 (always counts as 1 dc), work 2 dc over ring, ch 2, *work 3 dc over ring, ch 2; rep from * 3 times. Join rnd with a sl st in 3rd ch of ch-3. Fasten off. From WS, join D with a sl st in any ch-2 sp.

Rnd 2 Ch 3, work 2 dc in same ch-2 sp, ch 1, *work (3 dc, ch 2, 3 dc) in next ch-2 sp, ch 1; rep from * 3 times, end with 3 dc in beg ch-2 sp, ch 2. Join rnd with a sl st in 3rd ch of ch-3. Fasten off. From RS, join A with a sl st in any ch-2 sp.

Rnd 3 Ch 1 (counts as 1 sc), work 2 sc in same ch-2 sp, cont to sc in each st around, working 3 sc in each corner. Join rnd with a sl st in ch-1. From WS, join C with a sl st in any corner st.

Rnd 4 Rep rnd 3. From RS, join B with a sl st in any corner st.

Rnd 5 Rep rnd 3. Fasten off leaving a long tail for sewing.

EARFLAPS

With C, ch 5. **Row 1 (WS)** Sc in 2nd ch from hook and in next 2 ch, work 2 sc in last ch. Turn to bottom lps of beg ch, sc in next 4 lps—9 sts. Join B, ch 1, turn.

Row 2 Sc in first 4 sts, work 3 sc in next st (corner made), sc in last 4 sts. Join A, ch 1, turn.

Row 3 Sc in each st around, working 3 sc in center st of corner. Join E, ch 1, turn.

Row 4 Rep row 3. Join D, ch 1, turn.

Row 5 Rep row 3. Join C, ch 1, turn.

Row 6 Rep row 3. Join B, ch 1, turn.

Row 7 Rep row 3. Join A, ch 1, turn.

Row 8 Rep row 8. Fasten off. Turn to straight edge of earflap. From RS, join D with a sc in top right edge.

Row 1 Making sure that work lies flat, sc evenly across. Join E, ch 1, turn.

Row 2 Sc in each st across. Join B, ch 1, turn.

Row 3 Rep row 2. Fasten off.

FINISHING

Working through back lps, sew crown to brim.

Hat edging

From RS, join F with a sc in any st at bottom edge of brim.

Rnd 1 Sc in each st around. Join rnd with a sl st in first st. Fasten off.

Earflap edging

From RS, join F with a sc in right bottom edge.

Row 1 Making sure that work lies flat, sc evenly around to left bottom edge. Fasten off.

Seam trim

Trim is worked in chain st. Take care to maintain gauge as you work. Position hat so crown/brim seam is at top and RS is facing you. Make a slip knot in end of F. Insert hook between first and 2nd sts to the left of one seam. On WS, place slip knot on hook and draw up to RS. Insert hook between 2nd and 3rd sts and draw up a lp, then draw through lp on hook—first chain st made. Insert hook between 3rd and 4th sts and draw up a lp, then draw through lp on hook—2nd chain st made. Working from right to left, cont in chain st around entire seam. Fasten off. Working in the same manner, work chain st along each seam of brim. Sew on earflaps.

Ties

(make 2)

Cut one 13"/33cm-length each of A, B, C and E, and 2 lengths of D. Knot strands tog at one end. Braid strands, then knot opposite end. Sew ties to WS of earflaps.

*C*hase away the chills with a gorgeous shearling-inspired jacket accented with a cozy faux-fur collar and cuffs and a whimsical tassel on the zipper. Top it with the dapper helmet hat with earflaps, and you'll transform an outfit from ordinary to extraordinary.

golden child

JACKET

SIZES

Instructions are written for size 6 months. Changes for sizes 12 months and 18 months are in parentheses.

FINISHED MEASUREMENTS

- Chest (closed) 24 (26, 27½)"/61 (66, 70)cm
- Length 11 (12, 13)"/28 (30.5, 33)cm
- Upper arm 10 (11, 12)"/25.5 (28, 30.5)cm

MATERIALS

- *4 (5, 5) 1¾oz/50g balls (each approx 120yd/110m) of Berroco, Inc.'s **Suede** (nylon) in #3714 hopalong cassidy (MC)*  **4**
- *1 1¾oz/50g ball (approx 90yd/83m) of Berroco, Inc.'s **Berroco Plush** (nylon) in #1901 crema (CC)* **5**
- *Size H/8 (5mm) crochet hook or size to obtain gauge*
- *Yarn needle*
- *9 (10, 10½)"/23 (25.5, 26.5)cm-long separating zipper*
- *Matching sewing thread*
- *Sewing needle*
- *2½"/6.5cm square piece of cardboard (for tassel)*

GAUGE

14 sts and 17 rows to 4"/10cm over sc using size H/8 (5mm) hook and MC. Take time to check gauge.

NOTE

It's sometimes difficult to see the sts when working with furry yarn. For best results, count sts as you work across each row to make sure you do not skip or miss a st.

BACK

With MC, ch 43 (47, 49). **Row 1 (WS)** Sc in 2nd ch from hook and in each ch across—42 (46, 48) sts. Ch 1, turn. **Row 2** Sc in each st across. Ch 1, turn. Rep row 2 for pat st and work even until piece measures 10½ (11½, 12½)"/26.5 (29, 31.5)cm from beg, end with a WS row.

Right neck shaping

Next row (RS) Work across first 15 (16, 17) sts, ch 1, turn. Work one more row; piece should measure 11 (12, 13)"/28 (30.5, 33)cm from beg. Fasten off.

Left neck shaping

Next row (RS) Sk 12 (14, 14) center sts, join MC with a sc in next st, work to end. Ch 1, turn. Work one more row. Fasten off.

Work as for left front reversing shaping.

SLEEVES

With MC, ch 22 (24, 27). **Row 1 (RS)** Sc in 2nd ch from hook and in each ch across—21 (23, 26) sts. Ch 1, turn. Work in sc and inc 1 st each side on next row, then every 3rd row 6 (7, 7) times more—35 (39, 42) sts. Work even until piece measures 7 (8, 9)"/17.5 (20.5, 23)cm from beg. Fasten off.

FINISHING

Sew shoulder seams. Place markers 5 (5¹/₂, 6)"/12.5 (14, 15)cm down from shoulder seams on fronts and back. Sew sleeves to armholes between markers. Sew side and sleeve seams.

Edging

With RS facing, join MC with a sc in left shoulder seam. **Rnd 1** Making sure that work lies flat, sc evenly around neck, fronts and bottom edges, working 3 sc in each corner. Join rnd with a sl st in first st. Fasten off. For sleeves, join MC with a sc in sleeve seam. **Rnd 1** Making sure that work lies flat, sc evenly around bottom edge. Join rnd with a sl st in first st. Fasten off.

Front and bottom trim

With RS facing, join CC with a sc in top left front edge. **Row 1** Sc in each st around to top right front edge, working 3 sc in each corner. Ch 2, turn. **Row 2** Working in same

LEFT FRONT

With MC, ch 22 (24, 25). **Row 1 (WS)** Sc in 2nd ch from hook and in each ch across—21 (23, 24) sts. Ch 1, turn. Work even in sc until piece measures 9 (10, 10¹/₂")/23 (25.5, 26.5)cm from beg, end with a WS row.

Neck shaping

Next row (RS) Work across first 19 (20, 21) sts. Ch 1, turn. Dec 1 st at neck edge on next row, then every row 3 times more—15 (16, 17) sts. Work even until same length as back. Fasten off.

MC st as row 1, hdc in each st around, working 2 hdc in center st of each corner. Fasten off.

Collar

From RS, sk first st of right front neck, join CC with a hdc in next st. **Row 1** Hdc in each st across neck to within last st of left front neck. Ch 2, turn. **Rows 2, 3 and 4** Work 2 hdc in first st, hdc in each st to within last st, work 2 hdc in last st. Ch 2, turn. **Row 5** Hdc in each st across. Fasten off.

Cuffs

From RS, join CC with a sl st in first st at sleeve seam. **Rnd 1** Ch 2, hdc in each st around. Join rnd with a sl st in first ch of ch-2. Ch 2, turn. **Rnd 2** Hdc in each st around, inc 2 sts evenly spaced. Join rnd with a sl st in first ch of ch-2. Ch 2, turn. **Rnds 3 and 4** Hdc in each st around. Join rnd with a sl st in first ch of ch-2. After rnd 4 is completed, do not ch, fasten off. Fold back cuffs.

Embroidery

Use one strand of CC in needle throughout and refer to photo. For stitching detail around sleeve, beg at underarm seam. Working around last row of sleeve, sew running stitches (going under one st and over one st). For horizontal line of stitching on back, measure 1 (1½, 2)"/2.5 (4, 5)cm from beg of armhole. Sew running stitches from armhole edge to armhole edge. Rep horizontal lines on each front. Sew in zipper.

Tassel

Wrap MC 19 times around cardboard. Slip a 10"/25.5cm-length of MC under strands and tightly knot at one end of cardboard. Remove cardboard. Wrap and tie another length of yarn around the tassel about ½"/1.5cm down from the top. Cut loops at opposite ends. Trim ends even. Attach tassel to zipper pull.

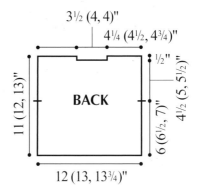

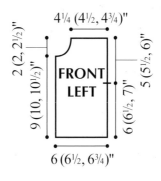

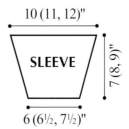

GAUGE

12 sts and 12 rnds to 4"/10cm over hdc using size H/8 (5mm) hook and MC.
Take time to check gauge.

CROWN

With MC, ch 50. Taking care not to twist ch, join ch with a sl st forming a ring. **Rnd 1 (RS)** Hdc in same ch as joining, then hdc in each ch around—50 sts. Join rnd with a sl st in first st. Ch 2, turn (back seam). **Rnd 2** Hdc in each st around. Join rnd with a sl st in first st. Ch 2, turn. Rep rnd 2 until 9 rnds have been completed. Next rnd Working in back lps only, hdc in each st around. Join rnd with a sl st in first st. Ch 2, turn.

HAT

SIZE

One size fits 6–18 months.

FINISHED MEASUREMENTS

• Circumference 16½"/42cm

MATERIALS

• 1 1¾oz/50g ball (approx 120yd/110m) of Berroco, Inc.'s **Suede** (nylon) in #3714 hopalong cassidy (MC) 【4】

• 1 1¾oz/50g ball (approx 90yd/83m) of Berroco, Inc.'s. **Berroco Plush** (nylon) in #1901 crema (CC) 【5】

• Size H/8 (5mm) crochet hook or size to obtain gauge

• Yarn needle

Crown shaping

Dec rnd 1 *Hdc in next 3 sts, dec 1 st over next 2 sts; rep from * around—40 sts. Join rnd with a sl st in first st. Ch 2, turn. **Dec rnd 2** Rep last rnd—32 sts. Join rnd with a sl st in first st. Ch 2, turn. **Dec rnd 3** *Hdc in next 2 sts, dec 1 st over next 2 sts; rep from * around—24 sts. Join rnd with a sl st in first st. Ch 2, turn. **Dec rnd 4** Rep last rnd—18 sts. Join rnd with a sl st in first st. Ch 2, turn. **Dec rnd 5** *Hdc in next st, dec 1 st over next 2 sts; rep from * around—12 sts. Join rnd with a sl st in first st. Ch 2, turn. **Dec rnd 6** [Dec 1 st over next 2 sts] 6 times—6 sts. Fasten off leaving a long tail. Thread tail into yarn needle and weave through sts. Pull tight to gather, fasten off securely.

Back flap

With bottom edge of hat at top, count 5 sts to the right of back seam. Join MC with a hdc in bottom lp of beg ch, cont working in bottom lps, hdc in next 10 lps. Ch 2, turn—11 sts. Working in hdc, work even for 3 more rows. Fasten off.

Right earflap

From RS, count 1 st to the left of back flap. Join MC with a hdc in bottom lp of beg ch, hdc in next 11 lps. Ch 2, turn—12 sts. **Row 1** Dec 1 st over first 2 sts, hdc in next 8 sts, dec 1 st over last 2 sts—10 sts. Ch 2, turn. **Row 2** Hdc in each st across. Ch 2, turn. **Row 3** Dec 1 st over first 2 sts, hdc in next 6 sts, dec 1 st over last 2 sts—8 sts. Ch 2, turn. **Row 4** Hdc in each st across. Ch 2, turn. **Row 5** Dec 1 st over first 2 sts, hdc in next 4 sts, dec 1 st over last 2 sts—6 sts. Ch 2, turn. **Row 6** Dec 1 st over first 2 sts, hdc in next 2 sts, dec 1 st over last 2

sts—4 sts. Ch 2, turn. **Row 7** [Dec 1 st over next 2 sts] twice—2 sts. Fasten off.

Left earflap

From RS, count 13 sts to the right of back flap. Join MC with a hdc in bottom lp of beg ch, hdc in next 11 lps. Ch 2, turn—12 sts. Cont to work as for right ear flap.

Bill

From RS, count 1 st to the left of right ear flap. Join CC with a hdc in bottom lp of beg ch, hdc in next 10 lps. Ch 2, turn—11 sts. **Row 2** Hdc in each st across. Ch 2, turn. **Row 3** Dec 1 st over first 2 sts, hdc in next 7 sts, dec 1 st over last 2 sts—9 sts. Ch 2, turn. **Row 4** Dec 1 st over first 2 sts, hdc in next 5 sts, dec 1 st over last 2 sts—7 sts. Ch 2, turn. **Row 5** Dec 1 st over first 2 sts, hdc in next 3 sts, dec 1 st over last 2 sts—5 sts. Fasten off.

FINISHING

Hat edging

From RS, join CC with a hdc in next st from left edge of bill. Making sure that work lies flat, hdc evenly around entire edge to next st from right edge of bill. Fasten off.

Bill edging

From WS, join MC with a hdc in RH edge of row 2. Making sure that work lies flat, hdc up right edge, across top edge and down left edge to LH edge of row 2. Fasten off. Fold up bill to RS and tack in place.

Ties

(make 2)

With CC, ch 23. **Row 1** Hdc in 3rd ch from hook and in each ch across—21 sts. Fasten off. Sew ties to earflaps, as shown.

W ho needs to sacrifice style for comfort? At the heel of fashion, this up-to-the-minute

footwear was inspired by the popular Australian sheepskin boots called Uggs.

These one-of-a-kind booties are easy to whip up in single and half double crochet.

feet first

Instructions are written for size 6–12 months.
Changes for size 12–18 months are in parentheses.

MATERIALS

- *1 1oz/50g ball (each approx 120yd/110m) of Berroco, Inc.'s **Suede** (nylon) each in #3717 wild bill hickcock (A) and #3714 hopalong cassidy (B)* **4**
- *1 1³⁄₄oz/50g ball (approx 90yd/83m) of Berroco, Inc.'s **Berroco Plush** (nylon) in #1901 crema (C)* **5**
- *For size 6–12 months, size G/6 (4mm) crochet hook or size to obtain gauge*
- *For size 12–18 months, size H/8 (5mm) crochet hook or size to obtain gauge*
- *1 small safety pin*
- *Yarn needle*

GAUGES

- 16 sts and 19 rows to 4"/10cm over sc using size G/6 (4mm) hook and A.
- 14 sts and 17 rows to 4"/10cm over sc using size H/8 (5mm) hook and A.

Take time to check gauges.

BOOTIE

Beg at center bottom of sole, with size G/4mm (H/8mm) hook and A, ch 14.

Rnd 1 Sc in 2nd ch from hook, sc in next 9 ch, hdc in next ch, work 2 hdc in next ch, 3 hdc in last ch. Turn to bottom lps of beg ch. Work 2 hdc in each of first 2 lps, hdc in next lp, sc in next 9 lps, work 2 sc in last lp—32 sts. Mark last st made with the safety pin. You will be working in a spiral (to rnd 12) marking the last st made with the safety pin to indicate end of rnd.

Rnd 2 Work 2 sc in next st, sc in next 12 sts, [work 2 sc in next st, sc in next st] 3 times, sc in next 11 sts, 2 sc in next st, sc in next st—37 sts.

Rnd 3 Work 2 sc in next st, sc in next 13 sts, [work 2 sc in next st, sc in next st] twice, [sc in next st, 2 sc in next st] twice, sc in next 13 sts, work 2 sc in next st, sc in next st—43 sts.

Rnd 4 Working in back lps only, sc in each st around. Change to B.

Rnd 5 Sc in each st around.

Rnd 6 Sc in next 16 sts, [dec 1 st over next 2 sts, sc in next st] 4 times, sc in next 15 sts—39 sts.

Rnd 7 Sc in next 15 sts, [dec 1 st over next 2 sts] 5 times, sc in next 14 sts—34 sts.

Rnd 8 Sc in next 14 sts, hdc in next 2 sts, working in hdc, dec 1 st over next 2 sts, hdc in next 2 sts, sc in next 14 sts—33 sts.

Rnd 9 Sc in next 13 sts, hdc in next 2 sts, working in hdc, dec 1 st over next 2 sts, hdc in next 2 sts, sc in next 14 sts—32 sts.

Rnd 10 Sc in next 13 sts, [working in hdc, dec 1 st over next 2 sts] 3 times, sc in next 13 sts—29 sts.

Rnd 11 Working in sc, sc in next 10 sts, [dec 1 st over next 2 sts] twice, sc in next st, [dec 1 st over next 2 sts] twice, sc next 10 sts—25 sts. Drop safety pin. Join rnd with a sl st in next st. Ch 2, turn.

Rnds 12, 13, 14 and 15 Hdc in each st around. Join rnd with a sl st in first st. Ch 2, turn. After rnd 15 is completed, change to C, ch 2, turn.

Rnd 16 Hdc in each st around. Join rnd with a sl st in first st. Fasten off.

FINISHING

Embroidery

Use one strand of CC in needle throughout and refer to photo. For vertical stitching lines on each side of bootie, measure 1"/2.5cm from center front. Working from rnd 15, sew running stitches (going over one rnd and under next rnd) to rnd 5. For horizontal stitching line across instep, beg at one vertical stitching line at rnd 8. Sew running stitches (going over one st and under next st) to opposite side.

A plush faux-fur coat caters only to those who want to live on the cutting edge of style! Dimensional novelty yarn lends maximum texture, and single crochet stitch will have you whipping it up in a flash.

f u r   e v e r

Instructions are written for size 6 months. Changes for sizes 12 months and 18 months are in parentheses.

FINISHED MEASUREMENTS

- Chest (buttoned) 22 (24, 26)"/56 (61, 66)cm
- Length 11 (12, 13)"/28 (30.5, 33)cm
- Upper arm 10 (11, 12)"/25.5 (28, 30.5)cm

MATERIALS

- *4 (4, 5) 1³⁄₄oz/50g balls (each approx 60yd/54m) of Lion Brand Yarn's **Fun Fur** (polyester) in #206 confetti*

- *Size I/9 (5.5mm) crochet hook or size to obtain gauge*
- *3 ³⁄₄"/19mm buttons*

GAUGE

11 sts and 10 rows to 4"/10cm over sc using size I/9 (5.5mm) hook.

Take time to check gauge.

NOTE

It's sometimes difficult to see the sts when working with furry yarn. For best results, count sts as you work across each row to make sure you do not skip or miss a st.

BACK

Ch 31 (35, 37).

Row 1 Sc in 2nd ch from hook and in each ch across—30 (34, 36) sts. Ch 1, turn.

Row 2 Sc in each st across. Ch 1, turn. Rep row 2 for pat st and work even until piece measures 11 (12, 13)"/26.5 (28, 30.5, 33)cm from beg. Fasten off.

LEFT FRONT

Ch 17 (19, 20).

Row 1 Sc in 2nd ch from hook and in each ch across—16 (18, 19) sts. Ch 1, turn. Work even in sc until piece measures 7 (7½, 8)"/17.5 (19, 20.5)cm from beg.

Neck shaping

Next row Dec 1 st at beg of row, then at same edge 4 (5, 5) times more—11 (12, 13) sts. Work even until same length as back. Fasten off.

RIGHT FRONT

Work as for left front reversing neck shaping.

SLEEVES

Ch 17 (19, 21).

Row 1 Sc in 2nd ch from hook and in each ch across—16 (18, 20) sts. Ch 1, turn. Work in sc and inc 1 st each side on next row, then every other row 5 times more—28 (30, 32) sts. Work even until piece measures 7 (8, 9)"/17.5 (20.5, 23)cm from beg. Fasten off.

FINISHING

Sew shoulder seams. Place markers 5 (5½, 6)"/12.5 (14, 15)cm down from shoulder seams on fronts and back. Sew sleeves to armholes between markers. Sew side and sleeve seams.

Button loops

(make 3)

Ch 8. Fasten off leaving a long tail for sewing. Fold ch in half to make loop. On right front, sew first loop at beg of neck shaping and the rest spaced 2"/5cm apart. Sew on buttons.

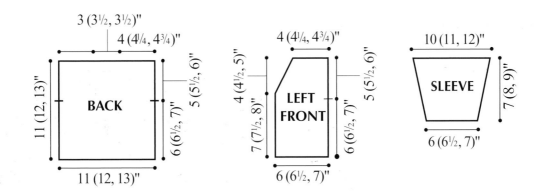

eet treats—stitch up your favorite playtime pals on a pair of cutie booties that are sure to draw smiles! From bunnies to ducks, bears to dinosaurs, these whimsical creatures—worked in single and half double crochet stitch—are a blast to wear.

h o t   s t e p

SIZES

Instructions are written for size 6–12 months.

Changes for size 12–18 months are in parentheses.

MATERIALS

• 1¾oz/50g balls of sportweight yarn in wool or wool blend **3**

Dinosaurs

• 1 ball in bright green (MC)

Bears

• 1 ball in medium brown (MC) and 5yd/5m each in off white (A) and black (B)

Bunnies

• 1 ball in pink (MC) and 5yd/5m in white (CC)

Ducks

• 1 ball in yellow (MC), 5yd/5m in orange (A) and 1yd/1m in black (B)

• For size 6–12 months, size F/5 (3.75mm) crochet hook or size to obtain gauge

• For size 12–18 months, size G/6 (4mm) crochet hook or size to obtain gauge

• 1 small safety pin

• Yarn needle

• 4 8mm sew-on wiggle eyes for each pair of booties

GAUGES

• 16 sts and 19 rows to 4"/10cm over sc using size F/5 (3.75mm) hook.

• 14 sts and 17 rows to 4"/10cm over sc using size G/6 (4mm) hook.

Take time to check gauges.

BASIC BOOTIE

Beg at center bottom of sole, with size F/3.75mm (G/4mm) hook and MC, ch 14. **Rnd 1** Sc in 2nd ch from hook, sc in next 9 ch, hdc in next ch, work 2 hdc in next ch, 3 hdc in last ch. Turn to bottom lps of beg ch. Work 2 hdc in each of first 2 lps, hdc in next lp, sc in next 9 lps, work 2 sc in last lp—32 sts. Mark last st made with the safety pin. You will be working in a spiral (to rnd 12) marking the last st made with the safety pin to indicate end of rnd.

Rnd 2 Work 2 sc in next st, sc in next 12 sts, [work 2 sc in next st, sc in next st] 3 times, sc in next 11 sts, 2 sc in next st, sc in next st—37 sts.

Rnd 3 Work 2 sc in next st, sc in next 13 sts, [work 2 sc in next st, sc in next st] twice, [sc in next st, 2 sc in next st] twice, sc in next 13 sts, work 2 sc in next st, sc in next st—43 sts.

Rnd 4 Working in back lps only, sc in each st around.

Rnd 5 Sc in each st around.

Rnd 6 Sc in next 16 sts, [dec 1 st over next 2 sts, sc in next st] 4 times, sc in next 15 sts—39 sts.

Rnd 7 Sc in next 15 sts, [dec 1 st over next 2 sts] 5 times, sc in next 14 sts—34 sts.

Rnd 8 Sc in next 14 sts, hdc in next 2 sts, working in hdc, dec 1 st over next 2 sts, hdc in next 2 sts, sc in next 14 sts—33 sts.

Rnd 9 Sc in next 14 sts, hdc in next 2 sts, working in hdc, dec 1 st over next 2 sts, hdc in next 2 sts, sc in next 14 sts—32 sts.

Rnd 10 Sc in next 14 sts, [working in hdc, dec 1 st over next 2 sts] twice, sc in next 14 sts—30 sts.

Rnd 11 Sc in next 12 sts, [working in sc, dec 1 st over next 2 sts] 3 times, sc next 12 sts—27 sts. Drop safety pin. Join rnd with a sl st in next st. Ch 2, turn.

Rnds 12, 13, 14 and 15 Hdc in each st around. Join rnd with a sl st in first st. Ch 2, turn. After rnd 15 is completed, do not ch, fasten off.

DINOSAURS

Using MC, make 2 basic booties.

Scales

(make 4)

With MC, ch 10. **Row 1** Sc in 2nd ch from hook, [work (hdc, 2 dc, hdc) in next ch, sk next ch, sc in next ch] once more, end work (hdc, 2 dc, hdc) in next ch, sl st in last ch. Fasten off leaving a long tail for sewing.

FINISHING

Sew a scale to front and back of each bootie; as shown. Sew on eyes.

BEARS

Using MC, make 2 basic booties.

Ears

(make 4)

With A, ch 4. Join ch with a sl st forming a ring.

Row 1 Work 6 sc over ring. Change to MC, ch 3, turn.

Row 2 Dc in first 2 sts, work 2 dc in each of next 2 sts, dc in last 2 sts. Fasten off leaving a long tail for sewing.

Sew on ears and eyes.

Embroidery

Use a single strand of B in yarn needle. Embroider nose in satin stitch, lip in straight stitch and mouth in stem stitch; as shown.

BUNNIES

Using MC, make 2 basic booties.

Ears

(make 4)

With CC, ch 10. **Row 1** Sc in 2nd ch from hook and in next 7 ch, work 5 sc in last ch. Turn to bottom lps of beg ch. Sk first lp, sc in each of 8 lps. Join MC, ch 2, turn. **Row 2** Hdc in first 10 sts, work 3 hdc in next st, hdc in last 10 sts. Fasten off leaving a long tail for sewing.

FINISHING

Sew on ears and eyes.

Embroidery

Use a single strand of CC in yarn needle. Embroider nose in satin stitch; as shown.

Tails

Using MC, make two 2"/5cm in diameter pompoms (see pompom instructions).

Sew a pompom to back of each bootie, as shown.

DUCKS

Using MC, make 2 basic booties.

Bills

(make 2)

With A, ch 7. **Row 1 (WS)** Sc in 2nd ch from hook and in each ch across—6 sts. Ch 1, turn. **Row 2** Working in sc, dec 1 st over first 2 sts, sc in next 2 sts, dec 1 st over last 2 sts—4 sts. Ch 1, turn. **Row 3** Working in sc, [dec 1 st over next 2 sts] twice—2 sts. Fasten off.

Edging From RS, join A with a sc in side edge of row 1. Making sure that work lies flat, sc evenly around edge to row 1 on opposite side. Fasten off leaving a long tail for sewing.

FINISHING

Sew on eyes.

Embroidery

Use a single strand of B in yarn needle. Embroider nostrils in straight stitch as shown. Sew on bills; as shown.

emerald isle

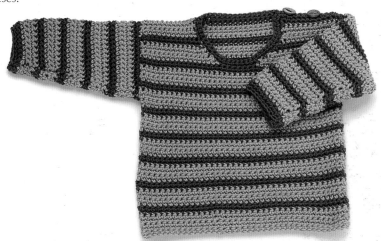

old stripes in eye-popping hues add plenty of verve to this quick-stitch sensation. A relaxed silhouette makes for an easy fit, while the matching pants provide all-day comfort.

SIZES

Instructions are written for size 6 months. Changes for sizes 12 months and 18 months are in parentheses.

FINISHED MEASUREMENTS

Pullover

- Chest 22 (24, 26)"/56 (61, 66)cm
- Length 11 (12, 13)"/28 (30.5, 33)cm
- Upper arm 9 (10, 11)"/23 (25.5, 28)cm

Pants

- Waist 21 (24, 26)"/53.5 (61, 66)cm
- Length 15 (16¹/₂, 18)"/38 (42, 45.5)cm

MATERIALS

Pullover

- 2 1³/₄oz/50g balls (each approx 108yd/100m) of Tahki Yarns/ Tahki•Stacy Charles, Inc.'s **Cotton Classic** (cotton) in #3715 green (A)
- 2 balls in #3786 teal (B)

Pants

- 2 balls each in #3715 green (A) and #3786 teal (B)
- Size G/6 (4mm) crochet hook or size to obtain gauge
- 2 ³/₄"/19mm buttons
- ³/₄yd/.75m of ¹/₂"/13mm-wide elastic
- White sewing thread
- Sewing needle

GAUGE

15 sts and 20 rows to 4"/10cm over sc using size G/6 (4mm) hook.
Take time to check gauge.

NOTE

See page 194 for how to work color changes for rows.

STRIPE PATTERN I

Working in sc, work 4 rows A and 2 rows B.
Rep these 6 rows for stripe pat I.

STRIPE PATTERN II

Working in sc, work 2 rows A and 2 rows B.
Rep these 4 rows for stripe pat II.

PULLOVER

BACK

With A, ch 43 (45, 49). **Row 1 (WS)** Sc in 2nd ch from
hook and in each ch across—42 (44, 48) sts. Ch 1, turn.
Beg with 2nd A row, cont in stripe pat I and work even
until piece measures 11 (12, 13)"/28 (30.5, 33)cm from
beg. Fasten off.

FRONT

Work as for back until piece measures 9 (10, 11)"/23
(25.5, 28)cm from beg, end with a WS row.

Left neck shaping

Next row (RS) Work across first 18 (19, 20) sts, ch 1,
turn. Dec 1 st from neck edge every row 3 (3, 2) times,
then every other row twice—13 (14, 16) sts. Work even
until piece measures same length as back. Fasten off.

Right neck shaping

Next row (RS) *Sk 6 (6, 8) center sts, join color in
progress with a sc in next st, work to end. Cont to work
as for left neck, reversing shaping.*

SLEEVES

With B, ch 23 (25, 27). **Row 1 (RS)** Sc in 2nd ch from
hook and in each ch across—22 (24, 26) sts. Beg with
2nd B row, cont in stripe pat I and inc 1 st each side
every 4th row 6 (7, 8) times—34 (38, 42) sts. Work even
until piece measures 7 (8, 9)"/17.5 (20.5, 23)cm from beg.
Fasten off.

FINISHING

Sew right shoulder seam.

Neck edging/buttonhole band

From RS, join B with a sc in first st of left front shoulder,
then sc in each st to within last st, work 2 sc in last st.
Making sure that work lies flat, sc evenly around front
neck edge, then cont along back neck and back left
shoulder. Ch 1, turn. **Next row** Sc in each st across to
left front shoulder, work 2 sc in corner, sc in next 1
(2, 2) sts, ch 2, sk next st, sc in next 4 (5, 6) sts, ch 2, sk
next st, sc in each st to end. Fasten off. Sew on buttons.
Fasten buttons into buttonholes, then pin left shoulder
to secure overlap. Place markers 4$\frac{1}{2}$ (5, 5$\frac{1}{2}$)"/11.5
(12.5, 14)cm down from shoulders on front and back.
Sew sleeves to armholes between markers. Sew side
and sleeve seams.

PANTS

LEFT LEG

With A, ch 29 (33, 35). **Row 1 (RS)** Sc in 2nd ch from
hook and in each ch across—28 (32, 34) sts. Ch 1, turn.

Beg with 2nd

A row, cont in stripe pat II and inc 1 st each side on next row, then every 3rd row 10 (11, 12) times more—50 (56, 60) sts. Work even until piece measures 7 (8, 9)"/17.5 (20.5, 23)cm from beg. Fasten off. Turn work.

Crotch shaping

Next row Sk first 2 sts, join color in progress with a sc in next st, work across to within last 2 sts. Ch 1, turn—46 (52, 56) sts. Dec 1 st each side every row 3 times—40 (46, 50) sts. Work even until piece measures 15 (16½, 18)"/38 (42, 45.5)cm from beg. Fasten off.

RIGHT LEG

Work as for left leg.

FINISHING

Sew front, back and leg seams. Measure waist and add 1"/2.5cm. Cut elastic to measurement. For casing for elastic, fold top edge of pants ¾"/2cm to WS and sew in place leaving a 1"/2.5cm opening at center back. Insert elastic through casing. Sew ends of elastic tog. Sew opening closed.

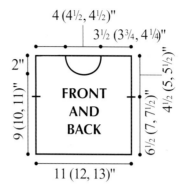

FRONT AND BACK

4 (4½, 4½)"
3½ (3¾, 4¼)"
2"
9 (10, 11)"
4½ (5, 5½)"
6½ (7, 7½)"
11 (12, 13)"

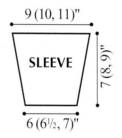

SLEEVE

9 (10, 11)"
7 (8, 9)"
6 (6½, 7)"

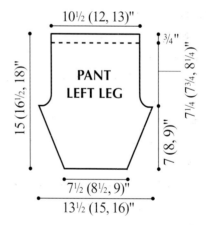

PANT LEFT LEG

10½ (12, 13)"
¾"
15 (16½, 18)"
7¼ (7¾, 8¼)"
7 (8, 9)"
7½ (8½, 9)"
13½ (15, 16)"

A button-front romper rendered in a refreshing palette of berry hues takes Baby from playtime to nap time in style. Enhanced with a striking trim, this snazzy handmade treasure is a treat to make and, more importantly, a delight to wear.

f i n e   l i n e s

SIZES

Instructions are written for size 6 months. Changes for sizes 12 months and 18 months are in parentheses.

FINISHED MEASUREMENTS

- Chest (buttoned) 22 (24, 26)"/56 (61, 66)cm
- Hips 26 (28, 31)"/66 (71, 78.5)cm
- Length 21 (25, 27½)"/53.5 (63.5, 70)cm
- Upper arm 9 (10, 11)"/23 (25.5, 28)cm

MATERIALS

- *3 (4, 4) 1³⁄₄oz/50g balls (each approx 108yd/100m) of Tahki Yarns/Tahki•Stacy Charles, Inc.'s **Cotton Classic** (cotton) each in #3003 ecru (A) and #3911 fuchsia (B)* 🧶**4**
- *1 ball in #3411 orange (C)*
- *Size G/6 (4mm) crochet hook or size to obtain gauge*
- *5 ⁵⁄₈"16mm buttons*

GAUGE

15 sts and 20 rows to 4"/10cm over sc using size G/6 (4mm) hook.

Take time to check gauge.

NOTE

See page 194 for how to work color changes for rows.

STRIPE PATTERN

Working in sc, work 6 rows A and 6 rows B. Rep these 12 rows for stripe pat.

LEFT LEG

With C, ch 27 (31, 35). **Row 1 (RS)** Sc in 2nd ch from hook and in each ch across—26 (30, 34) sts. Ch 1, turn. **Row 2** Sc in each st across. Ch 1, turn. Rep row 2 for pat st and work even for 2 more rows. Cont in stripe pat and inc 1 st each side on next row, then every other row 14 (14, 15) times more—56 (60, 66) sts. Work even until piece measures 7 (8, 9)"/17.5 (20.5, 23)cm from beg. Fasten off. Turn work.

Crotch shaping

Next row Sk first 2 sts, join color in progress with a sc in next st, work across to within last 2 sts. Ch 1, turn—52 (56, 62) sts. Dec 1 st each side every row twice—48 (52, 58) sts. Work one more row if necessary to end with a WS row. Fasten off.

RIGHT LEG

Work as for left leg. Sew front, back and leg seams.

BODY

From RS, join color in progress with a sc in first st, then sc in each st across—96 (104, 116) sts. Cont in stripe pat as established until piece measures 12 (14, 16)"/30.5 (35.5, 40.5)cm from beg, end with a WS row.

Waist shaping

Next row (RS) Sc in first 22 (24, 27) sts, [dec 1 st over next 2 sts] twice, sc in next 44 (48, 54) sts, [dec 1 st over next 2 sts] twice, sc in last 22 (24, 27) sts—92 (100, 112) sts. Work 3 rows even. **Next row (RS)** Sc in first 21 (23, 26) sts, [dec 1 st over next 2 sts] twice, sc in next 42 (46, 52) sts, [dec 1 st over next 2 sts] twice, sc in last 21 (23, 26) sts—88 (96, 108) sts. Work 3 rows even.

Next row (RS) Sc in first 20 (22, 25) sts, [dec 1 st over next 2 sts] twice, sc in next 40 (44, 50) sts, [dec 1 st over next 2 sts] twice, sc in last 20 (22, 25) sts—84 (92, 104) sts. Work 0 (3, 3) rows even.

For sizes 18 and 24 months only

Next row (RS) Sc in first 22 (24) sts, [dec 1 st over next 2 sts] 1 (2) times, sc in next 44 (48) sts, [dec 1 st over next 2 sts] 1 (2) times, sc in last 22 (24) sts—90 (100) sts.

For all sizes

Work even on 84 (90, 100) sts until piece measures 16½ (20, 22)"/42 (51, 56)cm from beg, end with a WS row. Mark last row for beg of armhole.

RIGHT FRONT

Next row (RS) Work across first 19 (20, 23) sts. Ch 1, turn. Work even until armhole measures 2½ (2½, 3)"/6.5 (6.5, 7.5)cm, end with a RS row.

Neck shaping

Next row (WS) Work across to within last 2 sts. Ch 1, turn. Dec 1 st at beg of next row, then at same edge every row 3 (3, 4) times more—13 (14, 16) sts. Work even until armhole measures 4½ (5, 5½)"/11.5 (12.5, 14)cm. Fasten off.

BACK

Next row (RS) Sk next 4 sts, join color in progress with a sc in next st, sc across next 37 (41, 45) sts. Ch 1, turn—38 (42, 46) sts. Work even until back measures same length as right front. Fasten off.

LEFT FRONT

Next row (RS) Sk next 4 sts, join color in progress with a sc in next st, sc to end. Ch 1, turn—19 (20, 23) sts. Cont to work same as for right front, reversing neck shaping.

SLEEVES

With C, ch 25 (27, 29). **Row 1 (RS)** Sc in 2nd ch from hook and in each ch across—24 (26, 28) sts. Ch 1, turn. Work in sc for 3 more rows. Join A, ch 1, turn. Cont in stripe pat and inc 1 st each side on next row, then every 4th row 4 (5, 6) times more—34 (38, 42) sts. Work even until piece measures 7½ (8½, 9)"/19 (21.5, 23)cm from beg. Fasten off.

FINISHING

Sew shoulder seams. Sew front crotch seam for 4 (5, 6)"/10 (12.5, 15)cm.

Front and neck bands

With RS of right front facing, join C with a sc above crotch seam. **Row 1** Making sure that work lies flat, sc evenly up right front edge, around neck edge, then down left front edge, working 3 sc in each corner st. Ch 1, turn. **Row 2** Sc in each st across, working 3 sc in each corner st. Ch 1, turn. Place markers on right front band for 5 buttons, with the first 2 sts from neck edge, the last 1"/2.5cm from top of crotch seam and the rest spaced evenly between. **Row 3 (buttonhole row)** *Sc in each st to marker, ch 2, sk next 2 sts; rep from * 5 times, then cont in sc to end, working 3 sc in each corner st. Ch 1, turn. **Row 4** Sc in each st across, working 2 sc in each ch-2 sp. Fasten off. Lap right front band over left and sew bottom edges of bands in place.

Collar

From RS, join C with a sc 1"/2.5cm from right front edge, sc in each st across to within 1"/2.5cm of left front edge. Ch 1, turn. Work in sc and inc 1 st each side on next row, then every other row twice more. Work even until collar measures 2½ (3, 3)"/6.5 (7.5, 7.5)cm from beg. Fasten off. Sew sleeve seams. Set in sleeves. Sew on buttons.

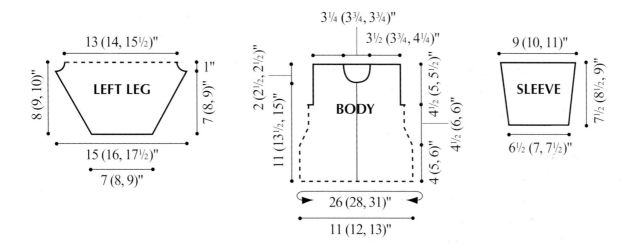

When the temperature drops, keep your little one toasty in this snazzy pullover-and-pant set. The pullover has running trellises of cables across the front and single crochet edging, while the pants offer an elastic waistband for all-day comfort.

warm front

Instructions are written for size 6 months. Changes for sizes 12 months and 18 months are in parentheses.

FINISHED MEASUREMENTS

Pullover

- Chest 21 (23, 25)"/53.5 (58.5, 63.5)cm
- Length 11 (11½, 12)"/28 (29, 30.5)cm
- Upper arm 9 (9½, 10)"/23 (24, 25.5)cm

Pants

- Waist 21 (24, 26)"/53.5 (61, 66)cm
- Length 15 (16½, 18)"/38 (42, 45.5)cm

MATERIALS

Pullover

- *4 (5, 5) 1¾oz/50g balls (each approx 136yd/125m) of Debbie Bliss/KFI's **Cashmerino Baby** (wool/ microfiber/cashmere) in #503 olive (A)* 3

Pants

- *3 (4, 4) balls in #203 teal (B)*
- *Size G/6 (4mm) crochet hook or size to obtain gauge*
- *3 ½"/13mm buttons*
- *¾yd/.75m of ½"/13mm-wide elastic*
- *White sewing thread*
- *Sewing needle*

GAUGES

- 20 sts and 17 rows to 4"/10cm over cable pat using size G/6 (4mm) hook.
- 16 sts and 16 rows to 4"/10cm over pat st using size G/6 (4mm) hook.

Take time to check gauges.

STITCH GLOSSARY

FPDC (Front Post Double Crochet)

Yo, working from front to back to front, insert hook around post of st of row below, yo and draw up a lp, [yo and draw through 2 lps on hook] twice.

BPDC (Back Post Double Crochet)

Yo, working from back to front to back, insert hook around post of st of row below, yo and draw up a lp, [yo and draw through 2 lps on hook] twice.

PATTERN STITCH

Row 1 *Sc in front lp of next st, sc in back lp of next st; rep from * to end. Ch 1, turn.

Rep row 1 for pat st.

CABLE TWIST

(Worked over 3 sts)

Row 1 (RS) Sk 2 sts, FPDC around next st, ch 1, FPDC around first sk st (leave 2nd st unworked).

Row 2 BPDC, sc in ch-1 sp, BPDC.

Rep rows 1 and 2 for cable twist.

PULLOVER

FRONT

With A, ch 54 (58, 62).

Foundation row 1 (RS) Sc in 2nd ch from hook and in each ch across—53 (57, 61) sts. Ch 1, turn.

Foundation row 2 Work row 1 of pat st. Ch 1, turn.

Beg pat sts

Row 1 (RS) Work pat st across first 5 (7, 9) sts, [work row 1 of cable twist over next 3 sts, work pat st across next 7 sts] 4 times, work row 1 of cable twist over next 3 sts, work pat st across last 5 (7, 9) sts. Ch 1, turn.

Row 2 Work pat st across first 5 (7, 9) sts, [work row 2 of cable twist over next 3 sts, work pat st across next 7 sts] 4 times, work row 2 of cable twist over next 3 sts, work pat st across last 5 (7, 9) sts. Ch 1, turn.

Row 3 Sc across first 5 (7, 9) sts, [work row 1 of cable twist over next 3 sts, sc across next 7 sts] 4 times, work row 1 of cable twist over next 3 sts, sc across last 5 (7, 9) sts. Ch 1, turn.

Row 4 Sc across first 5 (7, 9) sts, [work row 2 of cable twist over next 3 sts, sc across next 7 sts] 4 times, work row 2 of cable twist over next 3 sts, sc across last 5 (7, 9) sts. Ch 1, turn. Rep rows 1-4 until piece measures 7 (7½, 8)"/17.5 (19, 20.5)cm from beg, end with a WS row. Mark beg and end of last row for beg of neck opening.

LEFT FRONT

Next row (RS) Work across first 25 (27, 29) sts. Ch 1, turn. Work even until opening measures 2½"/6.5cm, end with a WS row.

Left neck shaping

Next row (RS) Work across first 21 (23, 25) sts. Ch 1, turn. Dec 1 st at beg of next row, then at same edge every row 5 times more—15 (17, 19) sts. Work even until piece measures 11 (11½, 12)"/28 (29, 30.5)cm from beg. Fasten off.

RIGHT FRONT

Next row (RS) Sk next 3 sts, join A with a sc in next st, work to end. Ch 1, turn—25 (27, 29) sts. Cont to work as for left front, reversing neck shaping.

BACK

With A, ch 54 (58, 62).

Foundation row 1 (RS) Sc in 2nd ch from hook and in

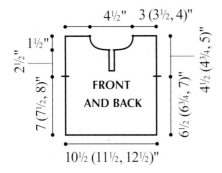

FRONT
AND BACK

4½" 3 (3½, 4)"

1½"

2½"

7 (7½, 8)"

6½ (6¾, 7)"

4½ (4¾, 5)"

10½ (11½, 12½)"

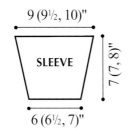

SLEEVE

9 (9½, 10)"

7 (7, 8)"

6 (6½, 7)"

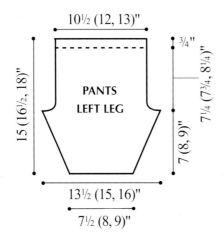

PANTS
LEFT LEG

10½ (12, 13)"

¾"

15 (16½, 18)"

7¼ (7¾, 8¼)"

7 (8, 9)"

13½ (15, 16)"

7½ (8, 9)"

each ch across—53 (57, 61) sts. Ch 1, turn.

Foundation row 2 Work row 1 of pat st across. Ch 1, turn.

Beg pat sts

Rows 1 and 2 Work in pat st. Ch 1, turn.

Rows 3 and 4 Sc in each st across. Ch 1, turn. Rep rows 1-4 until piece measures same length as front. Fasten off.

SLEEVES

With A, ch 32 (34, 36).

Foundation row 1 (RS) Sc in 2nd ch from hook and in each ch across—31 (33, 35) sts. Ch 1, turn.

Foundation row 2 Work row 1 of pat st across. Ch 1, turn.

Beg pat sts

Row 1 (RS) Work pat st across first 14 (15, 16) sts, work row 1 of cable twist over next 3 sts, work pat st across last 14 (15, 16) sts. Ch 1, turn.

Row 2 Work pat st across first 14 (15, 16) sts, work row 2 of cable twist over next 3 sts, work pat st across last 14 (15, 16) sts. Ch 1, turn.

Row 3 Sc across first 14 (15, 16) sts, work row 1 of cable twist over next 3 sts, sc across last 14 (15, 16) sts. Ch 1, turn.

Row 4 Sc across first 14 (15, 16) sts, work row 2 of cable twist over next 3 sts, sc across last 14 (15, 16) sts. Ch 1, turn. Rep rows 1-4 for pat sts. AT SAME TIME, working new sts into pat sts, inc 1 st each side every 4th row 7 times—45 (47, 49) sts. Work even until piece measures 7 (7, 8)"/17.5 (17.5, 20.5)cm from beg. Fasten off.

FINISHING

Sew shoulder seams.

Front and neck bands

With RS of right front facing, join A with a sc above neck opening.

Row 1 Making sure that work lies flat, sc evenly up right front edge, around neck edge, then down left front edge, working 3 sc in each corner st. Ch 1, turn. Place markers on right front for boy (or left front for girl) for 3 buttons, with the first 1 st from neck edge, the 2nd 2 sts from top of neck opening and the 3rd spaced evenly between.

Row 2 (buttonhole row) *Sc in each st to marker, ch 1, sk next st; rep from * twice more, then cont in sc to end, working 3 sc in each corner st. Ch 1, turn.

Row 3 Sc in each st across, working a sc in each ch-1 sp and working 3 sc in each corner st. Fasten off. Lap buttonhole band over button band and sew bottom edges of bands in place. Place markers 4$\frac{1}{2}$ (4$\frac{3}{4}$, 5)"/11.5 (12, 12.5)cm down from shoulder seams on front and back. Sew sleeves to armholes between markers. Sew side and sleeve seams. Sew on buttons.

Bottom edging

From RS, join A with a sl st in right side seam.

Rnd 1 Ch 1, making sure that work lies flat, sc evenly around edge. Join rnd with a sl st in first st.

Rnds 2 and 3 Ch 1, sc in each around. Join rnd with a sl st in first st. Fasten off.

Sleeve edging

From RS, join A with a sl st in underarm seam. Cont to work as for bottom edging.

PANTS

LEFT LEG

With B, ch 31 (33, 37).

Foundation row (RS) Sc in 2nd ch from hook and in each ch across—30 (32, 36) sts. Ch 1, turn. Cont in pat st and inc 1 st each side on next row, then every other row 11 (13, 13) times more—54 (60, 64) sts. Work even until piece measures 7 (8, 9)"/17.5 (20.5, 23)cm from beg. Fasten off. Turn work.

Crotch shaping

Next row Sk first 2 sts, join B with a sc in next st, work across to within last 2 sts. Ch 1, turn—50 (56, 60) sts. Dec 1 st each side every row 4 times—42 (48, 52) sts. Work even until piece measures 15 (16$\frac{1}{2}$, 18)"/38 (42, 45.5)cm from beg. Fasten off.

RIGHT LEG

Work as for left leg.

FINISHING

Sew front, back and leg seams. Measure waist and add 1"/2.5cm. Cut elastic to measurement. For casing for elastic, fold top edge $\frac{3}{4}$"/2cm to WS and sew in place leaving a 1"/2.5cm opening at center back. Insert elastic through casing. Sew ends of elastic tog. Sew opening closed.

his sweet short-sleeved dress and matching wrap are wearable on any occasion. Subtle lace-work, picot edging and a dainty white ribbon lend rustic appeal to the dress, while alternate rows of single and crossed double crochet stitches create the lovely pattern on the surplice.

summer love

DRESS AND WRAP

SIZES

Instructions are written for size 6 months. Changes for sizes 12 months and 18 months are in parentheses.

FINISHED MEASUREMENTS

Dress

- Chest 18 (20, 22)"/45.5 (51, 56)cm
- Length 14 (16, 18)"/35.5 (40.5, 45.5)cm
- Upper arm 8 (9, 10)"/20.5 (23, 25.5)cm

Wrap

- Chest (buttoned) 20 (22, 23½)"/51 (56, 59.5)cm
- Length 8½ (9½, 10)"/21.5 (24, 25.5)cm
- Upper arm 9 (10, 11)"/23 (25.5, 28)cm

MATERIALS

Dress

- *3 (4, 5) 1¾oz/50g balls (each approx 136yd/125m) of Debbie Bliss/KFI's **Cashmerino Baby** (wool/microfiber/cashmere) in #600 pink* (3)
- *Size F/5 (3.75mm) crochet hook or size to obtain gauge*
- *3 ½"/13mm buttons*
- *1¼yd/1.25m of ³⁄₁₆"/5mm-wide ivory satin ribbon*

Wrap

- *2 (2, 3) balls in #600 pink*
- *Size F/5 (3.75mm) crochet hook or size to obtain gauge*
- *3 ½"/13mm buttons*
- *2 medium snaps*
- *Matching sewing thread*
- *Sewing needle*

GAUGES

- 17 sts and 13 rows to 4"/10cm over hdc using size F/5 (3.75mm) hook.
- 17 sts and 18 rows to 4"/10cm over pat st using size F/5 (3.75mm) hook.

Take time to check gauges.

PATTERN STITCH

Rows 1–4 Sc in each st across. Ch 1, turn. After row 4 is completed, ch 3, turn.

Row 5 Dc in first st, *sk next st, dc in next st, dc in sk st; rep from *, end dc in last st. Ch 1, turn.

Rep rows 1–5 for pat st.

DRESS

NOTES

1 Back and front bodices are made separately, then sewn tog.

2 Skirt is made in one piece from bodice to hem.

BACK BODICE

Ch 40 (44, 48).

Row 1 (WS) Hdc in 3rd ch from hook and in each ch across—38 (42, 46) sts. Ch 2, turn.

Row 2 Hdc in each st across. Ch 2, turn. Rep row 2 and work even until piece measures 3 (3½, 4)"/7.5 (9, 10)cm from beg, end with a WS row. Fasten off. Turn work.

Armhole shaping

Next row (RS) Sk first 4 sts, join yarn with a hdc in next st, work across to within last 4 sts. Ch 2, turn—30 (34, 38) sts. Work even until armhole measures 4 (4½, 5)"/10 (11.5, 12.5)cm. Fasten off.

FRONT BODICE

Ch 39 (43, 47).

Row 1 Sc in 2nd ch from hook and in each ch across— 38 (42, 46) sts. Ch 1, turn. Beg with row 2, cont in pat st and work even until piece measures 3 (3½, 4)"/7.5 (9, 10)cm from beg, end with row 1, 2 or 5. Fasten off. Turn work.

Armhole shaping

Next row (RS) Sk first 4 sts, join yarn with a sc in next st, work across to within last 4 sts. Keeping to pat st, ch 1 or 3, turn—30 (34, 38) sts. Work even until armhole measures 2 (2½, 3)"/5 (6.5, 7.5)cm.

Left neck shaping

Next row (RS) Work across first 12 (13, 15) sts, ch 1 or 3, turn. Dec 1 st from neck edge every row 3 (3, 4) times—9 (10, 11) sts. Work even until piece measures same length as back. Fasten off.

Right neck shaping

Next row (RS) Sk 6 (8, 8) center sts, join yarn with a sc or dc in next st, work to end. Cont to work as for left neck, reversing shaping. Ch 1, turn.

Buttonhole band Sc in first 1 (2, 1) sts, [ch 1, sk next st, sc in next 2 (2, 3) sts] twice, ch 1, sk next st, sc in last st.

Next row Sc in each st across, working 1 sc in each ch-1 sp. Fasten off. Sew side seams.

SKIRT

From RS, join yarn with a sl st in right side seam.

Rnd 1 Ch 1, working through bottom lps of row 1, sc in each st around—76 (84, 92) sts. Join rnd with a sl st in first st; turn.

Rnd 2 Ch 2, *work 2 hdc in next st, hdc in next st; rep from * around—114 (126, 138) sts. Join rnd with a sl st in first st; turn.

Rnd 3 Ch 2, hdc in each st around. Join rnd with a sl st in first st; turn. Rep rnd 3 and work even until skirt measures 7 (8, 9)"/17.5 (20.5, 23)cm from beg, end with a WS row.

Picot row Sc in first 2 sts, *ch 3, sl st in 3rd ch from hook, sc in next 3 sts; rep from * around. Join rnd with a sl st in first st. Fasten off.

SLEEVES

Ch 32 (34, 36).

Row 1 (WS) Hdc in 3rd ch from hook and in each ch across—30 (32, 34) sts. Ch 2, turn. Work in hdc and inc 1 st each side on next row, then every 3rd row 1 (2, 3) times more—34 (38, 42) sts. Work even until piece measures 4 (4½, 5)"/10 (11.5, 12.5)cm from beg. Fasten off.

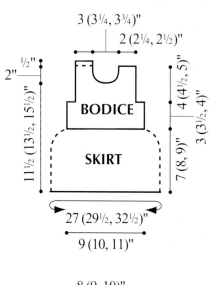

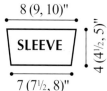

FINISHING

Sew left shoulder seam.

Neck edging

With RS of right back shoulder facing, sk first 9 (10, 11) shoulder sts, join yarn with a sc in next st. Making sure that work lies flat, work picot row around neck edge as foll: Sc in next st, *ch 3, sl st in 3rd ch from hook, sc in next 3 sts; rep from * to right front shoulder. Fasten off. Sew on buttons. Fasten buttons into buttonholes, then pin right shoulder to secure overlap. Sew sleeve seams. Set in sleeves.

Sleeve edging

From RS, join yarn with a sl st in underarm seam.

Row 1 Ch 1, working in bottom lps of row 1, sc in first 2 lps, *ch 3, sl st in 3rd ch from hook, sc in next 3 lps; rep from * around. Join rnd with a sl st in first sc. Fasten off. Weave ribbon through first row 5 of pat st on bodice, beg and ending at center front. Tie ribbon in a bow and trim ends at an angle.

WRAP

BACK

Ch 44 (48, 52).

Row 1 (WS) Hdc in 3rd ch from hook and in each ch across—42 (46, 50) sts. Ch 2, turn.

Row 2 Hdc in each st across. Ch 2, turn. Rep row 2 and work even until piece measures 4$^1/_2$ (5, 5)"/11.5 (12.5, 12.5)cm from beg, end with a WS row. Fasten off. Turn work.

Armhole shaping

Next row (RS) Sk first 4 sts, join yarn with a hdc in next st, work across to within last 4 sts. Ch 2, turn—34 (38, 42) sts. Work even until armhole measures 4 (4$^1/_2$, 5)"/10 (11.5, 12.5)cm. Fasten off.

LEFT FRONT

Ch 43 (47, 51).

Foundation row (WS) Sc in 2nd ch from hook and in each ch across—42 (46, 50) sts. Ch 1, turn. Cont in pat st and work even until 8 rows have been completed, end with a WS row.

Neck shaping

Next row (RS) Dec 1 st at end of row, then at same edge every row 27 (29, 31) times more. AT THE SAME TIME, when piece measures 4$^1/_2$ (5, 5)"/11.5 (12.5, 12.5)cm from beg, end with a WS row. Fasten off. Turn work.

Armhole shaping

Next row (RS) Sk first 4 sts, keeping to pat st join yarn with either a sc or dc, work to end. When all neck dec have been completed, work even on 10 (12, 14) sts until piece measures same length as back. Fasten off.

RIGHT FRONT

Ch 43 (47, 51).

Foundation row (WS) Sc in 2nd ch from hook and in each ch across—42 (46, 50) sts. Ch 1, turn. Cont in pat st and work buttonholes as foll:

Row 1 Sc in first st, ch 1, sk next st, sc in each st to end. Ch 1, turn.

Row 2 Sc in each st across, working one sc in ch-1 sp. Ch 1, turn.

Row 3 Sc in each st across. Ch 1, turn.

Row 4 (WS) Sc in each st to within last 2 sts, ch 1, sk next st, sc in last st. Ch 3, turn.

Row 5 Dc in first st, sk next ch-1 sp, dc in next st, dc in ch-1 sp, *sk next st, dc in next st, dc in sk st; rep from *, end dc in last st. Ch 1, turn.

Row 6 (WS) Rep row 4.

Row 7 Rep row 2. Ch 1, turn.

Row 8 Sc in each st across. Ch 1, turn. Cont to work as for left front, reversing shaping.

SLEEVES

Ch 28 (30, 32).

Row 1 (WS) Hdc in 3rd ch from hook and in each ch across—26 (28, 30) sts. Ch 2, turn. Work in hdc and inc 1 st each side on next row, then every 4th row 5 (6, 7) times more—38 (42, 46) sts. Work even until piece measures 8 (9, 10)"/20.5 (23, 25.5)cm from beg. Fasten off.

FINISHING

Sew shoulder seams.

Picot edging

From RS, join yarn with a sc in beg of right neck shaping.

Row 1 Making sure that work lies flat, sc evenly along entire neck edge to beg of left neck shaping. Ch 1, turn.

Row 2 Sc in each st across. Ch 1, turn.

Row 3 (RS) Sc in first 2 sts, *ch 3, sl st in 3rd ch from hook, sc in next 3 sts; rep from * to end. Fasten off. Set in sleeves. Sew side and sleeve seams. Sew on buttons. On RS of left front, sew one half of first snap set ½"/1.3cm from bottom edge and the 2nd snap at beg of neck shaping. On WS, sew other side of snap sets to left side seam.

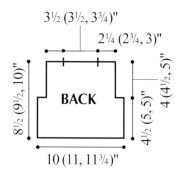

3½ (3½, 3¾)"
2¼ (2¾, 3)"
8½ (9½, 10)"
BACK
4 (4½, 5)"
4½ (5, 5)"
10 (11, 11¾)"

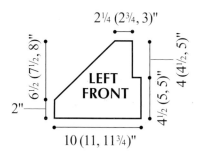

2¼ (2¾, 3)"
6½ (7½, 8)"
LEFT FRONT
4 (4½, 5)"
4½ (5, 5)"
2"
10 (11, 11¾)"

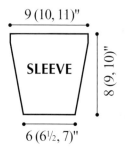

9 (10, 11)"
SLEEVE
8 (9, 10)"
6 (6½, 7)"

From sea to shore, this nautical pullover with matching shorts will keep your cabin boy at the helm of fashion. The crewneck pullover features vibrant stripes across the body and matching buttons along the left shoulder; elastic-waist pants keep this look casual.

a h o y ,   m a t e y !

Instructions are written for size 6 months. Changes for sizes 12 months and 18 months are in parentheses.

FINISHED MEASUREMENTS

Top

- Chest 20 (22, 24)"/51 (56, 61)cm
- Length 10½ (11½, 12½)"/26.5 (29, 31.5)cm
- Upper arm 8 (9, 10)"/20.5 (23, 25.5)cm

Shorts

- Waist 21 (24, 26)"/53.5 (61, 66)cm
- Length 11 (12, 12½)"/28 (30.5, 31.5)cm

MATERIALS

Top

- *2 (3, 3) 1¾oz/50g balls (each approx 136yd/125m) of Patons' **Grace** (mercerized cotton) in #60005 snow (A)*
- *1 ball each in #60705 cardinal (B) and #60134 royal (C)*

Shorts

- *3 (3, 4) balls in #60134 royal (C)*
- *Size F/5 (3.75mm) crochet hook or size to obtain gauge*
- *2 ⅞"/22mm red star buttons*
- *¾yd/.75m of ½"/13mm-wide elastic*
- *White sewing thread*
- *Sewing needle*

NOTE

One of the original colors used for this project is no longer available. The following substitution is recommended:

- *#60110 marine for #60134 royal (C)*

GAUGE

20 sts and 17 rows to 4"/10cm over hdc using size F/5 (3.75mm) hook.

Take time to check gauge.

NOTE

See page 194 for how to work color changes for rows.

Work 4 rows A in hdc and 2 rows B in sc. Rep these 6 rows for stripe pat.

TOP

BACK

With A, ch 52 (58, 62). **Row 1 (WS)** Hdc in 3rd ch from hook and in each ch across—50 (56, 60) sts. Ch 2, turn. **Rows 2–4** Hdc in each st across. Ch 2, turn. **Row 5** Rep row 2. Join B, ch 1, turn. **Rows 6 and 7** Sc in each st across. Ch 1, turn. When row 7 is completed, join A, ch 2, turn. Cont in stripe pat and work even until 4th B stripe has been completed. Cont with A and hdc until piece measures 6½ (7, 7½)"/16.5 (17.5, 19)cm from beg, end with a WS row. Fasten off. Turn work.

Armhole shaping

Next row Sk first 5 sts, join A with a hdc in next st, work across to within last 5 sts. Ch 2, turn—40 (46, 50) sts. Work even until armhole measures 4 (4½, 5)"/10 (11.5, 12.5)cm. Fasten off.

FRONT

Work as for back until armhole measures 2 (2½, 3)"/5 (6.5, 7.5)cm, end with a WS row.

Left neck shaping

Next row (RS) Work across first 17 (19, 20) sts, ch 2, turn. Dec 1 st from neck edge every row 5 times—12 (14, 15) sts. Work even until armhole measures 4 (4½, 5)"/10 (11.5, 12.5)cm, end with a WS row. Ch 1, turn.

Buttonhole band

Next (buttonhole) row (RS) Sc in first 3 (4, 4) sts, ch 2, sk next 2 sts, sc in next 4 (5, 6) sts, ch 2, sk next 2 sts, sc in last st. Ch 1, turn. **Next row** Sc across, working

2 sc in each ch-2 sp. Fasten off.

Right neck shaping

Next row (RS) Sk 6 (8, 10) center sts, join A with a hdc in next st, work to end. Cont to work as for left neck, reversing shaping, until armhole measures 4 (4½, 5)"/10 (11.5, 12.5)cm, end with a WS row. Fasten off.

SLEEVES

With A, ch 36 (38, 40). **Row 1 (WS)** Hdc in 3rd ch from hook and in each ch across—34 (36, 38) sts. Ch 2, turn. Work in hdc and inc 1 st each side on next row, then every 3rd row 2 (3, 5) times more—40 (44, 50) sts. Work even until piece measures 4 (4½, 5)"/10 (11.5, 12.5)cm from beg. Fasten off.

FINISHING

Sew right shoulder seam.

Button band

With RS of back facing, sk first 28 (32, 35) sts, join A with a sc in next, then sc in last 12 (14, 15) sts. Ch 1, turn. Cont to work in sc for one more row. Fasten off.

Neck edging

From RS, join C with a sl st in side edge of left front buttonhole band. Making sure that work lies flat, sc evenly along entire neck edge. Ch 1, turn. **Next row** Sc in each st across. Fasten off. Sew on buttons. Fasten buttons into buttonholes, then pin left shoulder to secure overlap. Set in sleeves, sewing last 1"/2.5cm at top of sleeve to armhole sts. Sew sleeve seams.

Sleeve edging

From RS, join C with a sl st in underarm seam. **Rnd 1** Ch 1, making sure that work lies flat, sc evenly around sleeve edge. Join rnd with a sl st in first st. **Rnd 2** Ch 1, sc in each st around. Join rnd with a sl st in first st. Fasten off.

SHORTS

LEFT LEG

With C, ch 52 (56, 62). **Row 1 (RS)** Hdc in 3rd ch from hook and in each ch across—50 (54, 60) sts. Ch 2, turn. Work in hdc and inc 1 st each side on next row, then every other row 2 (2, 3) times more, then every row 5 (6, 6) times—66 (72, 80) sts. Work even until piece measures 3 (3½, 4)"/7.5 (9, 10)cm from beg. Fasten off. Turn work.

Crotch shaping

Next row Sk first 2 sts, join C with a hdc in next st, work across to within last 2 sts. Ch 2, turn—62 (68, 76) sts. Dec 1 st each side every row 4 (5, 5) times—54 (58, 66) sts. Work even until piece measures 11 (12, 12½)"/28 (30.5, 31.5)cm from beg. Fasten off.

RIGHT LEG

Work as for left leg.

FINISHING

Sew front, back and leg seams. Measure waist and add 1"/2.5cm. Cut elastic to measurement. For casing for elastic, fold top edge of shorts ¾"/2cm to WS and sew in place leaving a 1"/2.5cm opening at center back. Insert elastic through casing. Sew ends of elastic tog. Sew opening closed.

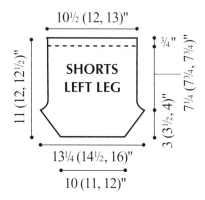

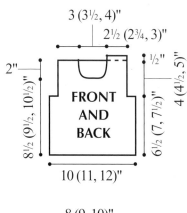

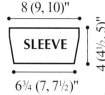

This all-American set makes for a memorable first salute to Independence Day. Celebrate the occasion in high spirits with a striped tank top and matching pants that would make Uncle Sam proud.

t a n k   g i r l

SIZES

Instructions are written for size 6 months. Changes for sizes 12 months and 18 months are in parentheses.

FINISHED MEASUREMENTS

Top

- Chest 20 (22, 24)"/51 (56, 61)cm
- Length 10 (11, 12)"/25.5 (28, 30.5)cm

Shorts

- Waist 21 (24, 26)"/53.5 (61, 66)cm
- Length 11 (12, 12½)"/28 (30.5, 31.5)cm

MATERIALS

Top

- *2 (3, 3) 1¾oz/50g balls (each approx 136yd/125m) of Patons' **Grace** (mercerized cotton) in #60005 snow (A)* 🧶**3**
- *1 ball each in #60134 royal (B) and #60705 cardinal (C)*

Shorts

- *3 (3, 4) balls in #60705 cardinal (C)*
- *Size F/5 (3.75mm) crochet hook or size to obtain gauge*
- *2 ⅞"/22mm red star buttons*
- *¾yd/.75m of ½"/13mm-wide elastic*
- *White sewing thread*
- *Sewing needle*

NOTE

One of the original colors used for this project is no longer available. The following substitution is recommended:

- *#60110 marine for #60134 royal (B)*

GAUGE

20 sts and 17 rows to 4"/10cm over hdc using size F/5 (3.75mm) hook.
Take time to check gauge.

NOTE

See page 194 for how to work color changes for rows.

Work 4 rows A in hdc and 2 rows B in sc.

Rep these 6 rows for stripe pat.

TOP

BACK

With A, ch 52 (58, 62). Row 1 (WS) Hdc in 3rd ch from hook and in each ch across—50 (56, 60) sts. Ch 2, turn. **Rows 2–4** Hdc in each st across. Ch 2, turn. **Row 5** Rep row 2. Join B, ch 1, turn. **Rows 6 and 7** Sc in each st across. Ch 1, turn. When row 7 is completed, join A, ch 2, turn. Cont in stripe pat and work even until 4th B stripe has been completed. Cont with A and hdc until piece measures 6½ (7, 8)"/16.5 (17.5, 20.5)cm from beg, end with a WS row. Fasten off. Turn work.

Armhole shaping

Next row Sk first 2 sts, join A with a hdc in next st, work across to within last 2 sts. Ch 2, turn—46 (52, 56) sts. Dec 1 st each side every row 3 (4, 4) times—40 (44, 48) sts. Work even until armhole measures 1½ (2, 2½)"/4 (5, 6.5)cm, end with a WS row.

Left neck shaping

Next row (RS) Work across first 17 (19, 21) sts, ch 2, turn. Dec 1 st from neck edge every row 5 (6, 7) times—12 (13, 14) sts. Work even until armhole measures 3½ (4, 4½)"/9 (10, 11.5)cm. Fasten off.

Right neck shaping

Next row (RS) Sk 6 center sts, join A with a hdc in next st, work to end. Cont to work as for left neck, reversing shaping.

FRONT

Work as for back.

FINISHING

Sew right shoulder seam.

Button band

From RS, join A with a sc in first st of left back shoulder, sc in next 11 (12, 13) sts. Ch 1, turn. Cont to work in sc for 2 more rows. Fasten off.

Buttonhole band

From RS, join A with a sc in first st of left front shoulder, sc in next 11 (12, 13) sts. Ch 1, turn. **Buttonhole row (WS)** Sc in first 1 (2, 2) sts, ch 2, sk next 2 sts, sc in next 5 (4, 5) sts, ch 2, sk next 2 sts, sc in last 1 (2, 2) sts. Ch 1, turn. **Next row Sc** across, working 2 sc in each ch-2 sp. Fasten off. Sew side seams.

Neck edging

From RS, join C with a sl st in side edge of left front buttonhole band. Making sure that work lies flat, sc evenly along entire neck edge. Ch 1, turn. **Next row** Sc in each st across. Fasten off.

Left armhole edging

From RS, join C with a sl st in side edge of left back button band. Making sure that work lies flat, sc evenly along entire armhole edge. Ch 1, turn. **Next row** Sc in each st across. Fasten off.

Right armhole edging

From RS, join C with a sl st in side seam. Making sure that work lies flat, sc evenly around armhole edge. Join rnd with a sl st in first st. Ch 1, turn. **Next rnd** Sc in each st around. Join rnd with a sl st in first st. Fasten off. Sew on buttons.

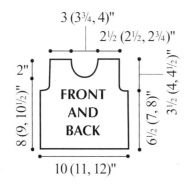

3 (3¾, 4)"

2½ (2½, 2¾)"

2"

**FRONT
AND
BACK**

8 (9, 10½)"

3½ (4, 4½)"

6½ (7, 8)"

10 (11, 12)"

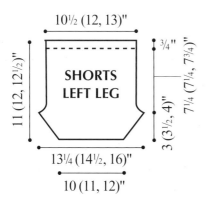

10½ (12, 13)"

¾"

11 (12, 12½)"

**SHORTS
LEFT LEG**

7¼ (7¼, 7¾)"

3 (3½, 4)"

13¼ (14½, 16)"

10 (11, 12)"

SHORTS

LEFT LEG

With C, ch 52 (56, 62). **Row 1 (RS)** Hdc in 3rd ch from hook and in each ch across—50 (54, 60) sts. Ch 2, turn. Work in hdc and inc 1 st each side on next row, then every other row 2 (2, 3) times more, then every row 5 (6, 6) times—66 (72, 80) sts. Work even until piece measures 3 (3½, 4)"/7.5 (9, 10)cm from beg. Fasten off. Turn work.

Crotch shaping

Next row Sk first 2 sts, join C with a hdc in next st, work across to within last 2 sts. Ch 2, turn—62 (68, 76) sts. Dec 1 st each side every row 4 (5, 5) times—54 (58, 66) sts. Work even until piece measures 11(12,12)"/28 (30.5, 31.5)cm from beg. Fasten off.

RIGHT LEG

Work as for left leg.

FINISHING

Sew front, back and leg seams. Measure waist and add 1"/2.5cm. Cut elastic to measurement. For casing for elastic, fold top edge of shorts ¾"/2cm to WS and sew in place leaving a 1"/2.5cm opening at center back. Insert elastic through casing. Sew ends of elastic tog. Sew opening closed.

Inspired by the traditional Chinese cheongsam, this darling dress features a single-crochet bodice trimmed in black and finished with a bountiful silk skirt. The complementary kimono jacket on p.125 makes an ideal cover-up.

east meets west

DRESS

SIZES

Instructions are written for size 6 months. Changes for sizes 12 months and 18 months are in parentheses.

FINISHED MEASUREMENTS

• Chest 20 (22, 24)"/51 (56, 61)cm

MATERIALS

• 2 1¾oz/50g balls (each approx 85yd/78m) of Berroco, Inc.'s **Cotton Twist** (mercerized cotton/rayon) in #8347 frankenberry (MC)

• 1 3oz/85g ball (approx 174yd/158m) of Lion Brand Yarn's **Lion Chenille** (acrylic) in #153 black (CC)

• Size H/8 (5mm) crochet hook or size to obtain gauge

• 1yd/1m of Asian print magenta satin fabric

• 2 small black frog fasteners

• Matching sewing threads

• Sewing needle

• Straight pins

GAUGE

14 sts and 16 rows to 4"/10cm over pat st using size H/8 (5mm) hook.

Take time to check gauge.

PATTERN STITCH

Row 1 Working through front lps only, sc in each st across. Ch 1, turn.

Rep row 1 for pat st.

BACK BODICE

With MC, ch 33 (37, 41).

Foundation row (RS) Sc in 2nd ch from hook and in each ch across—32 (36, 40) sts. Ch 1, turn. Cont in pat st and work even until piece measures 2½ (3, 3½)"/6.5 (7.5, 9)cm from beg, end with a WS row. Fasten off. Turn work.

Armhole shaping

Next row (RS) Sk first 3 sts, join MC with a sc in front lp of next st, work to within last 3 sts. Ch 1, turn—26 (30, 34) sts. Work even until armhole measures 3 (3½, 4)"/2.5 (4, 5)cm. Fasten off.

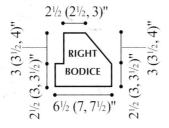

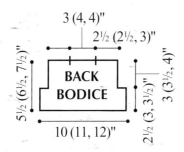

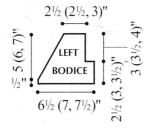

LEFT FRONT BODICE

With MC, ch 23 (25, 27).

Foundation row (RS) Sc in 2nd ch from hook and in each ch across—22 (24, 26) sts. Ch 1, turn. Cont in pat st for 2 rows, end with a RS row.

Neck shaping

Next row (WS) Dec 1 st at beg of row, then at same edge every other row 10 (11, 11) times more. AT SAME TIME, when piece measures 2½ (3, 3½)"/6.5 (7.5, 9)cm from beg, end with a WS row. Fasten off. Turn work.

Armhole shaping

Next row (RS) Sk first 3 sts, join MC with a sc in next st, work to end. Ch 1, turn. When neck shaping has been completed, work even on 8 (9, 11) sts until same length as back. Fasten off.

RIGHT FRONT BODICE

With MC, ch 23 (25, 27).

Foundation row (RS) Sc in 2nd ch from hook and in each ch across—22 (24, 26) sts. Ch 1, turn. Cont in pat st and work even until piece measures 2½ (3, 3½)"/6.5 (7.5, 9)cm from beg, end with a WS row.

Armhole shaping

Next row (RS) Work across to within last 3 sts. Ch 1, turn—19 (21, 23) sts.

Neck shaping

Next row (WS) Dec 1 st at end of row, then at same edge every row 10 (11, 11) times more—8 (9, 11) sts. Work even until same length as back. Fasten off.

FINISHING

Sew shoulder and side seams.

Edging

Lap right front over left front. On left front, use straight pins to mark where right front overlaps at neck and at bottom edge. Lift off right front. Move neck pin 2"/5cm down towards bottom edge and bottom pin 1"/2.5cm towards front edge. From RS, join CC with a sc at pin mark on left front bottom edge. Making sure that work lies flat, sc evenly around outer edge, working 2 sc in each corner and ending at pin mark on left front neck edge. Fasten off. Lap right front over left front and tack bottom edges tog where they overlap.

Armhole edging

From RS, join CC with a sc in underarm seam.

Rnd 1 Ch 1, making sure that work lies flat, sc evenly around armhole edge. Join rnd with a sl st in first sc. Fasten off.

Skirt

Cut a 30 (32, 36)"/76 (81, 91.5)cm by 20 (22, 23)"/51 (56, 58.5)cm piece of fabric. With RS tog and using 1/2"/13mm seam allowance, sew back seam. Gather one long edge of skirt, adjusting gathers to fit lower edge of bodice. Handsew skirt in place. Fold hem 1/4"/6mm to WS; press. Hem skirt to desired length. Sew on frogs.

JACKET

SIZES

Instructions are written for size 6 months. Changes for sizes 12 months and 18 months are in parentheses.

FINISHED MEASUREMENTS

- Chest (closed) 22 (24, 26)"/56 (61, 66)cm
- Length 11 (12, 13)"/28 (30.5, 33)cm
- Upper arm 8 (9, 10)"/20.5 (23, 25.5)cm

MATERIALS

- 3 (4, 5) 3oz/85g balls (each approx 174yd/158m) of Lion Brand Yarn's **Lion Chenille** (acrylic) in #153 black
  [4]
- Size H/8 (5mm) crochet hook or size to obtain gauge
- 1/2yd/.5m of Asian print magenta satin fabric
- 2 small black frog fasteners
- Matching sewing threads
- Sewing needle
- Straight pins

GAUGE

12 sts and 12 rows to 4"/10cm over hdc using size H/8 (5mm) hook.

Take time to check gauge.

Armhole shaping

Next row (RS) Sk first 3 sts, join yarn with a hdc in next st, work to within last 3 sts. Ch 2, turn—28 (30, 34) sts. Work even until armhole measures 4 (4½, 5)"/10 (11.5, 12.5)cm. Fasten off.

LEFT FRONT

Ch 24 (26, 28).

Row 1 (RS) Hdc in 3rd ch from hook and in each ch across—22 (24, 26) sts. Ch 2, turn. Work even in hdc until piece measures 7 (7½, 8)"/17.5 (19, 20.5)cm from beg, end with a WS row. Fasten off. Turn work.

Armhole and neck shaping

Next row (RS) Sk first 3 sts, join yarn with a hdc in next st, work across to within last 3 sts. Ch 2, turn—16 (18, 20) sts.

Neck shaping

Next row (WS) Dec 1 st at beg of row, then at same edge every row 6 (8, 9) times more—9 (9, 10) sts. Work even until same length as back. Fasten off.

RIGHT FRONT

Work as for left front, reversing shaping.

SLEEVES

Ch 20 (22, 24).

Row 1 (RS) Hdc in 3rd ch from hook and in each ch

BACK

Ch 36 (38, 42).

Row 1 (RS) Hdc in 3rd ch from hook and in each ch across—34 (36, 40) sts. Ch 2, turn.

Row 2 Hdc in each st across. Ch 2, turn. Rep row 2 for pat st and work even until piece measures 7 (7½, 8)"/17.5 (19, 20.5)cm from beg, end with a WS row. Fasten off. Turn work.

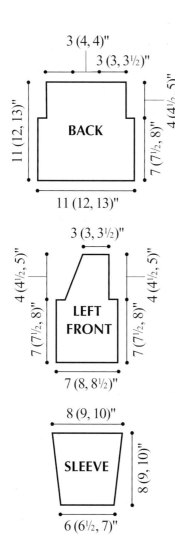

3 (4, 4)"

3 (3, 3½)"

11 (12, 13)"

BACK

4 (4½, 5)"

7 (7½, 8)"

11 (12, 13)"

3 (3, 3½)"

4 (4½, 5)"

4 (4½, 5)"

LEFT FRONT

7 (7½, 8)"

7 (7½, 8)"

7 (8, 8½)"

8 (9, 10)"

SLEEVE

8 (9, 10)"

6 (6½, 7)"

across—18 (20, 22) sts. Ch 2, turn. Work in hdc and inc 1 st each side on next row, then every 4th row 2 (3, 3) times more—24 (28, 30) sts. Work even until piece measures 8 (9, 10)"/20.5(23, 25.5)cm from beg. Fasten off.

FINISHING

Sew shoulder seams. Set in sleeves, sewing last 1"/2.5cm at top of sleeve to armhole sts. Sew side and sleeve seams.

Fabric trim

For fronts, necks and bottom edges, cut two strips of fabric 2"/5cm-wide by 31 (36, 42)"/78.5 (91.5, 106.5)cm-long. Sew short ends tog using a ½"/13mm seam; press seam open. Fold fabric strip in half lengthwise, WS facing; press. Fold each long edge ¼"/6mm to WS; press. Center seam at center back neck. Taking care to maintain st and row gauges, pin trim around entire edge, mitering trim around corners and ending at center back bottom. Trim excess fabric, leaving a 2"/5cm overlap. Fold each short edge 1"/2.5cm to WS, then overlap edges 1"/2.5cm. Working through all thicknesses, sew trim along top folded edges.

For cuffs, cut two strips of fabric 2"/5cm-wide by 8 (8½, 9)"/20.5 (21.5, 17.5)cm-long. Fold and press fabric strips same as for edging. Beg and ending at underarm seam, sew trim to sleeves. Sew on frogs.

simply mauve-olous

From Sunday school to preschool, dress her best in this adorable little design. Clever detailing such as the striped bodice, full skirt and cheerful daisy accent transform this dress into a stylish work of art.

SIZES

Instructions are written for size 3–6 months. Changes for sizes 9–12 months, 18–24 months and 3 years are in parentheses.

FINISHED MEASUREMENTS

- Chest 18 (20, 22, 24)"/45.5 (51, 56, 61)cm
- Length 14 (16, 19, 22)"/35.5 (40.5, 48, 56)cm

MATERIALS

- 3 (3, 3, 4) 3½oz/100g balls (each approx 205yd/187m) of Classic Elite Yarns' **Provence** (mercerized cotton) in #2654 english lilac (MC) 〔3〕
- 1 ball each in #2632 mad magenta (A), #2672 gentle green (B) and #2674 fiddlehead (C)
- Size H/8 (5mm) crochet hook or size to obtain gauge
- Small safety pin

NOTE

Two of the original colors used for this dress are no longer available. The following substitutions are recommended:
- #2636 citrine for #2672 gentle green (B)
- #2615 victory garden for #2674 fiddlehead (C)

GAUGE

16 sts and 16 rows to 4"/10cm over pat st 1 using size H/8 (5mm) hook.
Take time to check gauge.

NOTES

1 See page 194 for how to make color changes.
2 Front and back are made separately, then sewn tog.
3 Skirt is made in one piece from bodice to hem.

PATTERN STITCH 1

(over an even number of sts)

Row 1 *Sc into front lp of next st, sc into back lp of next st; rep from * across.

Ch 1, turn.

Rep row 1 for pat st 1.

PATTERN STITCH 2

(over an even number of sts)

Rnd 1 Ch 1, *sc into front lp of next st, sc into back lp of next st; rep from * around. Join rnd with a sl st in ch-1.

Rep rnd 1 for pat st 2.

STRIPE PATTERN

Working in pat st 1, work 2 rows each A, B, C and MC. Rep these 8 rows for stripe pat.

BACK BODICE

With MC, ch 37 (41, 45, 49).

Foundation row Sc in 2nd ch from hook and in each ch across—36 (40, 44, 48) sts. Ch 1, turn. Cont in pat st 1 for 1 row. Join A, ch 1, turn. Cont in stripe pat and work even until piece measures 1 (1½, 2, 2½)"/2.5 (4, 5, 6)cm from beg. Do not ch, turn.

Armhole shaping

Sl st across first 2 (2, 3, 3) sts, ch 1, work across to within last 2 (2, 3, 3) sts, ch 1, turn—32 (36, 38, 42) sts. Dec 1 st each side every row 2 (2, 2, 3) times—28 (32, 34, 36) sts. Work even until piece measures 2½ (3, 4, 4½)"/6 (7.5, 10, 11.5)cm from beg. Ch 1, turn.

Left neck shaping

Next row Work across first 11 (13, 13, 14) sts. Ch 1, turn. Dec 1 st from neck edge every row 3 (4, 4, 4) times—8 (9, 9, 10) sts. Work even until piece measures 4 (5, 6, 7)"/10 (12.5, 15, 17.5)cm from beg. Fasten off.

Right neck shaping

Next row Sk 6 (6, 8, 8) center sts, join yarn with a sc in next st, work to end. Cont to work as for left neck, reversing shaping.

FRONT BODICE

Work as for back bodice. Sew shoulder and side seams.

SKIRT

With RS facing, join MC with a sl st in left side seam.
Foundation rnd Ch 1, working in bottom lps of foundation ch, sc in each bottom lp around—72 (80, 88, 96) sts. Mark last st made with the safety pin to indicate end of rnd. Join rnd with a sl st in ch-1, changing to C.
Inc rnd *Work 2 sc in next st, sc in next st; rep from * around—108 (120,132,144) sts. Join rnd with a sl st in ch-1, changing to B. Cont in pat st 2 and work even for 2 rnds, changing to A after 2nd rnd. Work 2 rnds even, changing to MC after 2nd rnd. Cont to work even in pat st 2 until skirt measures 10 (11, 13, 15)"/25.5 (28, 33, 38)cm from beg. Fasten off.

FINISHING

Neck edging

With RS facing, join A with a sl st in left shoulder seam.
Rnd 1 Ch 1, making sure that work lies flat, sc evenly around. Join rnd with a sl st in ch-1. Fasten off.
Armhole edging

With RS facing, join A with a sl st in side seam.
Rnd 1 Ch 1, making sure that work lies flat, sc evenly around. Join rnd with a sl st in ch-1. Fasten off.

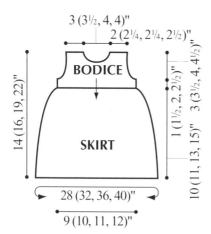

3 (3½, 4, 4)"
2 (2¼, 2¼, 2½)"
BODICE
14 (16, 19, 22)"
1 (1½, 2, 2½)"
3 (3½, 4, 4½)"
SKIRT
10 (11, 13, 15)"
28 (32, 36, 40)"
9 (10, 11, 12)"

It's off to the Emerald City! Show off her fashion sense in a snappy cotton argyle dress with colorful chain stitch patterning. A tiny ribbon threaded around the waist adds a pretty accent.

cross my heart

SIZES

Instructions are written for size 3–6 months. Changes for sizes 9–12 months, 18–24 months and 3 years are in parentheses.

FINISHED MEASUREMENTS

* Chest 18 (20, 22, 24)"/45.5 (51, 56, 61)cm
* Length 14 (15, 17, 18)"/35.5 (38, 43, 45.5)cm

MATERIALS

ORIGINAL YARN

* 3 (4, 4, 5) 1¾oz/50g balls (approx 136yd/124m) of Patons' **Grace** (mercerized cotton) in #60724 teal (MC)
* 1 ball each in #60723 aqua (A) and #60711 apple (B)

SUBSTITUTE YARN

* 4 (5, 6, 7) 1¾oz/50g balls (each approx 123yd/111m) of Reynolds/JCA's **Saucy Sport** (mercerized cotton) in #604 jungle teal (MC)
* 1 ball each in #247 pucci (A) and #63 parakeet green (B)
* Size G/6 (4mm) crochet hook or size to obtain gauge
* 11 bobbins
* Small safety pin
* 1½yd/1.5m of ¼"/6mm apple green satin ribbon

GAUGE

20 sts and 20 rows to 4"/10cm over pat st using size G/6 (4mm) hook.

Take time to check gauge.

NOTES

1 Front and back are made separately, then sewn tog.

2 Skirt is made in one piece from bodice to hem.

3 See page 195 for how to work color changes for argyle patterns.

4 Wind MC onto 5 bobbins and A and B onto 3 bobbins each.

5 See page 196 for how to embroider chain stitch.

PATTERN STITCH 1

Row 1 Sc in back lp of each st across. Ch 1, turn.

Rep row 1 for pat st 1.

PATTERN STITCH 2

Rnd 1 Ch 1, sc in back lp of each st around. Join rnd with a sl st in ch-1.

Rep rnd 1 for pat st 2.

BACK BODICE

With MC, ch 47 (51, 57, 61). **Foundation row** Sc in 2nd ch from hook and in each ch across—46 (50, 56, 60) sts. Ch 1, turn. Cont in pat st 1.

Beg chart 1 (1, 2, 2)

Row 1 Beg with st 3 (1, 3, 1) and work to st 48 (50, 58, 60). Cont to foll chart in this way until row 10 (10, 16, 16) is completed. Fasten off. Turn work.

Armhole shaping

Row 11 (11, 17, 17) Keeping to chart pat, sk first 3 (3, 4, 4) sts, join yarn with a sc in next st, work across to within last 3 (3, 4, 4) sts. Ch 1, turn—40 (44, 48, 52) sts. Dec 1 st each side every row 2 (2, 3, 3) times—36 (40, 42, 46) sts. Work even until row 16 (16, 20, 20) is completed. Ch 1, turn.

Left neck shaping

Row 17 (17, 21, 21) Work across first 14 (16, 17, 19) sts, ch 1 turn. Dec 1 st from neck edge every row 4 (5, 3, 3) times, every other row 0 (0, 2, 3) times—10 (11, 12, 13) sts. Work even until row 26 (28, 36, 38) is completed. Fasten off.

Right neck shaping

Row 17 (17, 21, 21) Keeping to chart pat, sk 8 center sts, join yarn with a sc in next st, work to end. Cont to work as for left neck, reversing shaping.

FRONT BODICE

Work as for back bodice.

Embroidery

Referring to chart (1, 1, 2, 2), use MC and B to embroider chain-stitch diagonal lines on back and front. Sew shoulder and side seams.

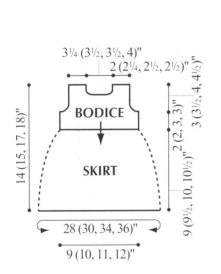

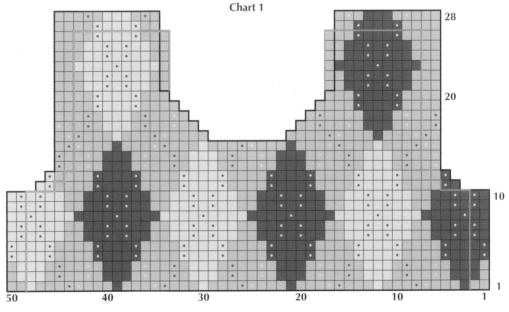

Chart 1

SKIRT

With RS facing, join MC with a sl st in left side seam.

Foundation rnd Ch 1, working in bottom lps of foundation ch, work 2 sc in each bottom lp around—92 (100, 112, 120) sts. Mark last st made with the safety pin to indicate end of rnd. Join rnd with a sl st in ch-1.

Inc rnd *Working through back lps, work 2 sc in next st, sc in next st; rep from * around—138 (150, 168, 180) sts. Join rnd with a sl st in ch-1. Cont in pat st 2 and work even until skirt measures 9 (9½, 10, 10½)"/23 (24, 25.5, 26.5)cm from beg.

Edging

Rnd 1 Ch 1, *sc in next st, ch 2, sk next st; rep from * around. Join rnd with a sl st in ch-1. Fasten off.

FINISHING

Neck edging

From RS, join MC with a sl st in left shoulder seam.

Rnd 1 Ch 1, making sure that work lies flat, sc around neck edge. Join rnd with a sl st in ch-1. Fasten off. Rep edging around each armhole. Beg and ending at center front, weave ribbon under and over sts of first rnd between bodice and skirt.

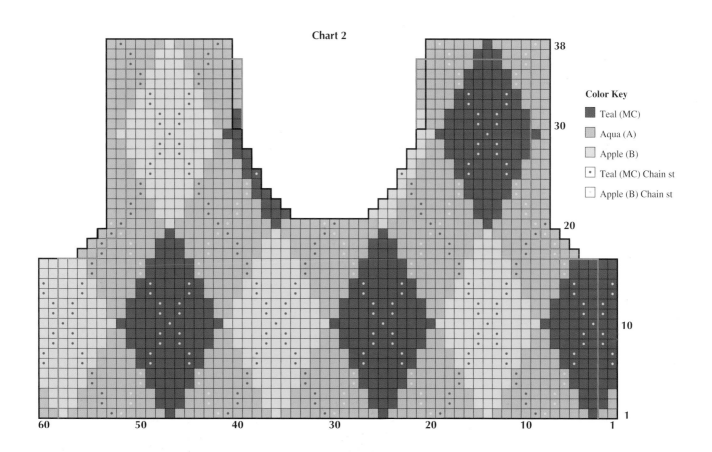

Chart 2

Color Key

- ■ Teal (MC)
- ■ Aqua (A)
- ■ Apple (B)
- ⊡ Teal (MC) Chain st
- ☐ Apple (B) Chain st

irls just want to have fun, and that's what this design is all about—she'll feel like a princess in this jewel-toned treasure. The shell stitched bodice is attached to a full-body skirt and then enhanced with a dazzling paillette trim along the empire waist.

holiday magic

SIZES

Instructions are written for size 3–6 months.
Changes for sizes 9–12 months, 18–24 months and
3 years are in parentheses.

FINISHED MEASUREMENTS

• Chest 18 (20, 22, 24)"/45.5 (51, 56, 61)cm

MATERIALS

• *2 (3, 3, 4) 1¾oz/50g balls (each approx 136yd/124m)
of Patons' **Grace** (mercerized cotton) in #60409 ruby*

3

• *Size F/5 (3.75mm) crochet hook or size to obtain gauge*
• *½ (⅔, 1, 1)yd/.5 (.75, 1, 1)m of 45"/114cm-wide
lavender dupioni silk*
• *1yd/1m of beaded fringe (optional)*
• *Matching sewing threads*

GAUGE

5 shells and 10 rows to 4"/10cm over pat st using size
F/5 (3.75mm) hook.
Take time to check gauge.

SHELL STITCH PATTERN

(multiple of 4 sts plus 1)

Row 1 Sc in first st, sk next st, *work 3 dc in next st (shell made), sk next st, sc in next st, sk next st; rep from *, end work 3 dc in next st (shell made), sk next st, sc in last st. Ch 3, turn.

Row 2 Work 2 dc in first sc (half shell made), sc in 3rd dc of next shell, *work 3 dc in next sc, sc in 3rd dc of next shell; rep from *, end work 2 dc in last sc. Ch 1, turn.

Row 3 Sc in first dc of half shell, *work 3 dc in next sc, sc in 3rd dc of next shell; rep from *, end work 3 dc in last sc, sc in 2nd dc of half shell. Ch 3, turn.

Rep rows 2 and 3 for pat st.

BACK BODICE

Ch 46 (50, 58, 62).

Foundation row Sc in 2nd ch from hook and in each ch across—45 (49, 57, 61) sts. Ch 1, turn. Work row 1 of pat st—11 (12, 14, 15) whole shells. Work row 2 of pat st—10 (11, 13, 14) whole shells and 2 half-shells. Cont in pat st and work even for 1 (3, 4, 6) rows, end ready for row 2 (2, 3, 3). Fasten off. Turn work.

Armhole shaping

Next row Sk first whole shell, join yarn with a sl st in next sc, ch 3, work 2 dc in same st (half shell), work to within sc of last whole shell, work 2 dc in this sc. Ch 1, turn—8 (9, 10, 11) whole shells and 2 half-shells. Beg with row 3 for all sizes, work even for 2 (4, 4, 4) rows, end ready for row 3.

Left neck shaping

Next row Sc in first dc of half shell, [work 3 dc in next sc, sc in 3rd dc of next shell] 2 (2, 3, 3) times. Ch 3, turn. Work even until armhole measures 3 (3½, 4, 4½)"/7.5 (9, 10, 11.5)cm. Fasten off.

Right neck shaping

Next row Sk 4 (5, 4, 5) center shells, join yarn with a sc in 3rd dc of next shell, work to end. Cont to work as for left neck.

FRONT BODICE

Work as for back bodice.

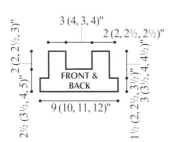

FINISHING

Sew shoulder and side seams. Cut beaded fringe to fit around lower edge of bodice, then add 1"/2.5cm for overlap. Hand-sew to WS of lower edge of bodice.

Skirt

From fabric, cut 2 skirt pieces each 15 (16, 18, 19)"/38 (40.5, 45.5, 48)cm x 20 (22, 23, 26)"/51 (56, 58.5, 66)cm. With RS tog and using ½"/13mm seam allowance sew side seams. Gather one long edge of skirt, adjust gathers to fit; hand-sew to lower edge of bodice. Press ¼"/6mm to WS along rem long edge of skirt, then hem to desired length.

nursery magic

That's a wrap—crochet goes contemporary with this extra-special blanket worked in easygoing shades. Inspired by the classic argyle design, the blanket boasts an assortment of various-sized squares, chain stitch embroidered accents and a single crochet border.

FINISHED MEASUREMENTS

- 34" x 34"/86.5 x 86.5cm

MATERIALS

- 5 3½oz/100g balls (each approx 205yd/187m) of Classic Elite Yarns' **Provence** (mercerized cotton) in #2674 fiddlehead (MC) [3]
- 3 balls in #2632 mad magenta (B)
- 1 ball each in #2648 slate blue (A) and #2603 morning mist (C)
- Size H/8 (5mm) crochet hook or size to obtain gauge
- Bobbins
- Yarn needle

NOTE

Two of the original colors used for this blanket are no longer available. The following substitutions are recommended:

- #2661 summer wheat for #2674 fiddlehead (MC)
- #2682 asparagus for #2603 morning mist (C)

GAUGES

- 14 sts and 12 rows to 4"/10cm over hdc using size H/8 (5mm) hook.
- One square to 10"/25.5cm using size H/8 (5mm) hook. Take time to check gauges.

NOTES

1 See page 194 for how to work color changes.

2 When working colorblock squares, wind MC onto 2 bobbins and A and B onto separate bobbins.

3 See page 196 for how to embroider chain stitch.

SOLID SQUARE

(make 4)

With MC, ch 38. Row 1 Hdc in 3rd ch from hook and in each ch across—36 sts. Ch 2, turn. Row 2 Hdc in each st across. Ch 2, turn. Rep row 2 until total of 30 rows have been completed. Fasten off.

COLORBLOCK SQUARE

(make 5)

With MC, ch 38, change to A.

Row 1 Hdc in 3rd ch from hook and in next 3 ch, with MC, hdc in next 28 ch, with A, hdc in last 4 ch—36 sts. Ch 2, turn.

Rows 2 and 3 With A, hdc in first 4 sts, with MC, hdc in next 28 sts, with A, hdc in last 4 sts. Ch 2, turn. After row 3 has been completed, join MC, ch 2, turn.

Rows 4–10 With MC, hdc in each st across. Ch 2, turn.

Rows 11–16 With MC, hdc in first 14 sts, with B, hdc in next 8 sts, with MC, hdc in last 14 sts. Ch 2, turn.

Rows 17–23 Rep rows 4–10. After row 23 is completed, join A, ch 2, turn.

Rows 24–26 Rep row 2. After row 26 is completed, do not ch, fasten off.

FINISHING

Lightly block squares to measurements. Referring to photo, sew squares tog.

Embroidery

Take care to maintain st and row gauge when working chain-stitches. Referring to photo, use C to embroider diagonal lines of chain-stitches as shown.

Border

From RS, join B with a sl st in any corner.

Rnd 1 Ch 1, making sure that work lies flat, sc evenly around, working 3 sc in each corner. Join rnd with a sl st in first sc.

Rnds 2–5 Ch 1, sc in each around, working 3 sc in each corner st. Join rnd with a sl st in first sc. Fasten off.

ariegated blocks in muted shades team up to lend a warm touch to this chic kiddie essential. Squares are stitched separately, then joined together and decorated with yellow stitching. A half double crochet border offers a handsome finish.

jean dream

FINISHED MEASUREMENTS

• 37" x 37"/94 x 94cm

MATERIALS

• 2 3½ oz/100g balls (each approx 196yd/180m) of Bernat's **Denimstyle** (acrylic/cotton) each in #3117 stonewash (A), #3044 sweatshirt (B) and #3108 indigo (C) 🔘4

• 1 ball (each approx 350yd/320m) of Aunt Lydia/Coats & Clark's **Classic Crochet Thread** (mercerized cotton) in #421 goldenrod (D) 🔘1

• Size I/9 (5.5mm) crochet hook or size to obtain gauge

• Yarn needle

GAUGES

• 10 sts and 7 rows to 4"/10cm over hdc using size I/9 (5.5mm) hook.

• One square to 11"/28cm using size I/9 (5.5mm) hook. Take time to check gauges.

NOTE

See page 194 for how to work color changes.

SQUARE

(make 9)

With A, ch 30.

Row 1 Hdc in 3rd ch from hook and in each ch across 28 sts. Ch 2, turn.

Row 2 Hdc in each st across. Ch 2, turn. Rep row 2 for pat st and work until a total of 19 rows have been completed. Fasten off. Make 2 more using A and 3 each using B and C.

FINISHING

Lightly block pieces to measurements. Referring to photo, sew squares tog.

Border

From RS, join A with a sl st in center of any side edge.

Rnd 1 Ch 2, making sure that work lies flat, hdc evenly around entire edge, working 3 hdc in each corner. Join rnd with a sl st in first hdc.

Rnd 2 Ch 2, hdc in each st around, working (2 hdc, ch 1, 2 hdc) in center hdc of each corner. Join rnd with a sl st in first hdc changing to B.

Rnds 3 and 4 Ch 2, hdc in each st around, working (2 hdc, ch 1, 2 hdc) in ch-1 sp of each corner. Join rnd with a sl st in first hdc. After rnd 4 is completed, join rnd with a sl st in first hdc changing to C.

Rnd 5 and 6 Rep rnd 3 and 4. After rnd 6 is completed, join rnd with a sl st in first hdc, fasten off.

Embroidery

Refer to photo. Use three strands of D in needle throughout and make sure to maintain st and row gauge when weaving. Working around rnd 1 of border, weave B under and over every 2 sts around. For vertical stitching lines, weave under and over each row between last 2 sts of RH and center squares, then between first 2 sts of center and LH squares. For horizontal stitching lines, weave under and over every 2 sts along row 18 of bottom and center row of squares, then along row 2 of center and top row of squares.

After a day of play, round up your little one with this fun crochet blanket. Achieve the look of denim with simple contrast stitching, combine it with a funky cow print, and your little wrangler can curl up in style.

cowboy blues

FINISHED MEASUREMENTS

• 30" x 34¾"/76 x 88cm (not including border)

MATERIALS

• 2 6oz/170g balls (each approx 290yd/265m) of TLC/Coats & Clark's **Amoré** (acrylic/nylon) in #3823 lake blue (A) 🔵4️⃣

• 1 ball each in #3001 white (B) and #3002 black (C)

• 1 ball (each approx 350yd/320m) of Aunt Lydia/Coats & Clark's **Classic Crochet Thread** (mercerized cotton) in #421 goldenrod (D) 🔵1️⃣

• Size H/8 (5mm) crochet hook or size to obtain gauge

• Bobbins

• Yarn needle

GAUGES

• 12 sts and 14 rows to 4"/10cm over sc and chart pat using size H/8 (5mm) hook.

• One block to 10" x 11½"/25.5 x 29cm using size H/8 (5mm) hook.

Take time to check gauges.

NOTES

1 Blanket can be made in one piece (version 1), as shown, or in separate blocks (version 2).

2 See page 194 for how to work color changes.

3 Wind B and C onto three separate bobbins each.

4 If making blanket in one piece, use a separate skein of A when working each A block.

and sc across next 30 sts, change to A and sc in last 30 sts. Ch 1, turn. Cont to work as established until row 40 of chart has been completed. Ch 1, turn. **Row 121** With A, sc in each st across. Fasten off.

VERSION 2

SOLID BLOCKS

(make 5)

With A, ch 31.

Row 1 (RS) Sc in 2nd ch from hook and in each ch across—30 sts. Ch 1, turn.

Row 2 Sc in each st across. Ch 1, turn. Rep row 2 for pat st and work until a total of 40 rows have been completed. Fasten off.

COW-PRINT BLOCKS

(make 4)

With B, ch 7, change to C and ch 16, change to B and ch 8.

Row 1 (RS) With B, sc in 2nd ch from hook and in next 6 ch, with C, sc in next 16 ch, with B, sc in last 7 ch—30 sts. Ch 1, turn.

Beg chart

Row 2 (WS) Working in sc (with a ch 1 to turn), beg at st 30 and work to st 1. Cont to work as established to row 40. Fasten off.

FINISHING

Lightly block piece or blocks to measurements.

Pocket embroidery

Use four strands of D in needle throughout and make sure to maintain st and row gauge when stitching. Referring to chart and photo, embroider each A block using running stitches. Referring to photo, sew blocks tog for version 2.

VERSION 1

ONE PIECE

With A, ch 91. **Row 1 (RS)** Sc in 2nd ch from hook and in next 29 ch, change to B and beg chart at st 1 on row 1 and work in sc across next 30 ch, change to A and sc in last 30 ch—90 sts. Ch 1, turn. **Row 2** With A, sc in first 30 sts, change to B and work row 2 of chart, change to A and sc in last 30 sts. Ch 1, turn. Cont to work as established until row 40 of chart has been completed. Change to B, ch 1, turn. **Row 41** With B, beg chart at st 1 on row 1 and work in sc across next 30 sts, change to A and sc in next 30 sts, with B, beg chart at st 1 on row 1 and work in sc across last 30 sts. Ch 1, turn. Cont to work as established until row 40 of chart has been completed. Change to A, ch 1, turn. **Row 81** With A, sc in first 30 sts, change to B, beg chart at st 1 on row 1

Border

From RS, join A with a sl st in any corner. **Rnd 1** Ch 1, making sure that work lies flat, sc evenly around entire edge, working 3 sc in each corner. Join rnd with a sl st in first sc. **Rnds 2–6** Ch 1, sc in each around, working 3 sc in each corner st. Join rnd with a sl st in first sc. Rnd 7 Ch 1, working from left to right, sc in each st around, working 2 sc in each corner st. Join rnd with a sl st in first sc. Fasten off.

Border embroidery

Use four strands of D in needle throughout and make sure to maintain st and row gauge when weaving. Working around rnd 1 of border, weave D under and over each st around, as shown. Rep weaving around rnd 3.

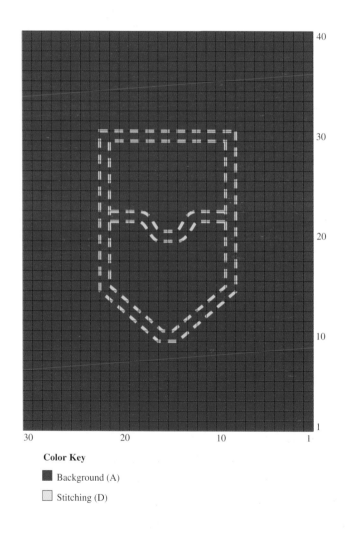

Color Key

■ Background (A)

□ Stitching (D)

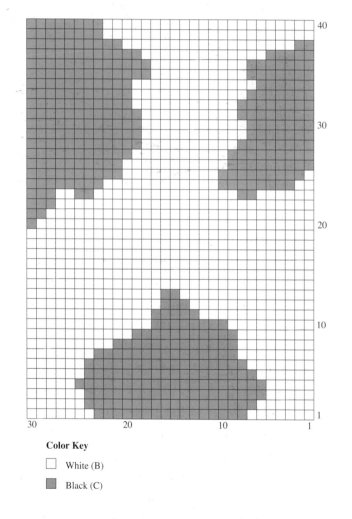

Color Key

□ White (B)

■ Black (C)

ooo-ve over, baby pastels, and make a bold statement with this cow-print blanket! A little intarsia makes for a fun, hip throw that will keep Baby warm all through the night.

creature comfort

FINISHED MEASUREMENTS

• 32" x 34¾"/81 x 88cm (not including border)

MATERIALS

• 2 6oz/170g balls (each approx 290yd/265m) of TLC/Coats & Clark's **Amoré** (acrylic/nylon) in #3001 white (A)

• 1 ball each in #3002 black (B) and #3823 lake blue (C)

• 1 ball (each approx 350yd/320m) of Aunt Lydia/ Coats & Clark's **Classic Crochet Thread** (mercerized cotton) in #421 goldenrod (D)

• Size H/8 (5mm) crochet hook or size to obtain gauge

• Bobbins

• Yarn needle

GAUGE

12 sts and 14 rows to 4"/10cm over sc and chart pat using size H/8 (5mm) hook.

Take time to check gauge.

NOTES

1 See page 194 for how to work color changes.

2 Wind A and B onto three separate bobbins each.

BLANKET

With A, ch 97.

Foundation row (WS) Sc in 2nd ch from hook and in each ch across—96 sts. Ch 1, turn.

Beg chart

Row 1 (RS) Working in sc (with a ch 1 to turn), beg at st 1 and work to st 96. Cont to work as established to row 120. Join A, ch 1, turn. Work even for 1 row. Fasten off.

FINISHING

Lightly block piece to measurements.

Border

From RS, join C with a sl st in any corner.

Rnd 1 Ch 1, making sure that work lies flat, sc evenly around entire edge, working 3 sc in each corner. Join rnd with a sl st in first sc.

Rnds 2–6 Ch 1, sc in each around, working 3 sc in each corner st. Join rnd with a sl st in first sc. After rnd 6 is completed, join rnd with a sl st in first sc, fasten off.

Embroidery

Use four strands of D in needle throughout and make sure to maintain st and row gauge when weaving. Working around rnd 3 of border, weave D under and over each st around, as shown. Rep weaving around rnd 5.

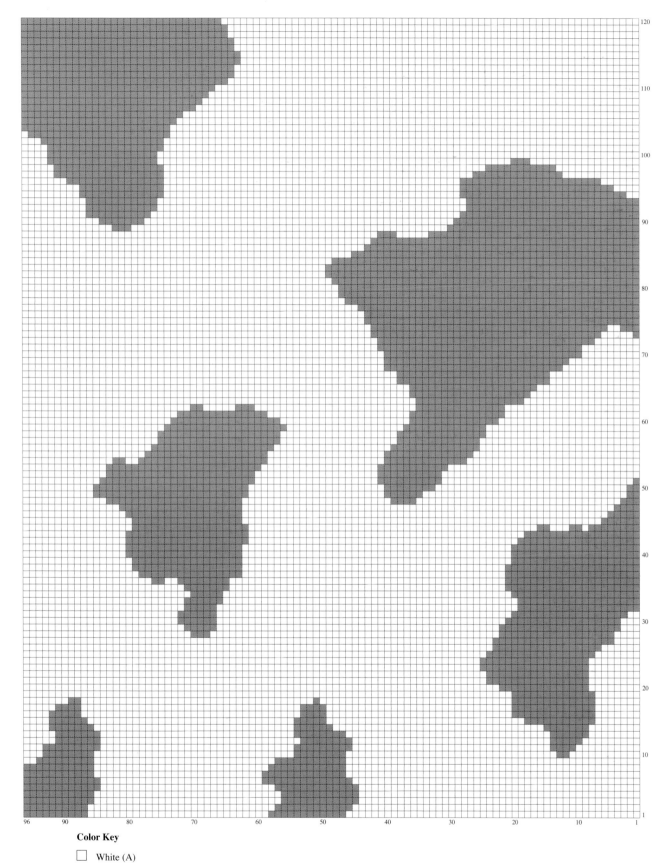

Color Key

☐ White (A)

■ Black (B)

This soft, cuddly blanket will have your baby smiling around the clock. Finishing touches like adorable crocheted ears and an embroidered smile make it an instant classic that any child will love, and its simple construction means you'll love it too!

bear necessity

FINISHED MEASURMENTS

• 35" x 35"/89 x 89cm

MATERIALS

• 3 1¼ oz/50g balls (each approx 114yd/105m) of Wendy/Berroco, Inc.'s **Velvet Touch** (nylon) in #1215 blue (C) **4**

• 2 balls each in #1200 white (A) and #2001 tan (B)

• Sportweight yarn in black for embroidery

• Size H/8 (5mm) crochet hook or size to obtain gauge

• Bobbins

• Yarn needle

NOTE

The original colors used for this blanket are no longer available. The following substitutions are recommended:

• #1245 ice blue for #1215 blue (C)

• #1200 white velvet for #1200 white (A)

• #1246 sahara velvet for #2001 tan (B)

GAUGES

• 12 sts and 10 rows to 4"/10cm over hdc using size H/8 (5mm) hook.

• One square to 9½"/24cm using size H/8 (5mm) hook. Take time to check gauges.

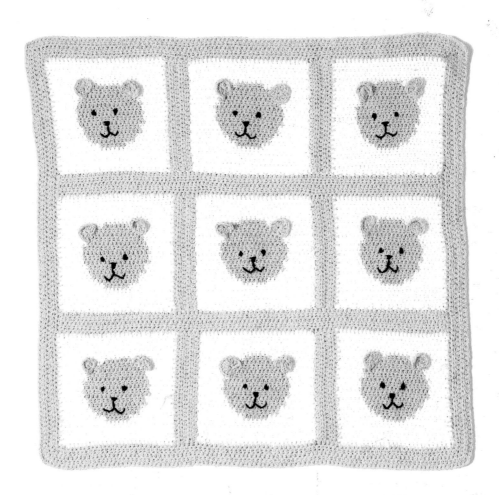

1 See page194 for how to work color changes.

2 Wind A onto two separate bobbins and B onto one bobbin.

SQUARE

(make 9)

With A, ch 30.

Row 1 (WS) Hdc in 3rd ch from hook and in each ch across—28 sts. Ch 2, turn.

Rows 2–5 Hdc in each st across. Ch 2, turn.

Beg chart

Row 6 (RS) Beg at st 1 and work to st 28. Work as established until row 24 is completed. Fasten off.

EARS

(make 18)

With B, ch 2.

Row 1 In 2nd ch from hook, work (sc, 2 hdc, dc, 2 hdc, sc). Ch 1, turn.

Row 2 Sc in first st, work 2 hdc in each of next 2 sts, dc in next st, work 2 hdc in each of next 2 sts, sc in last st. Fasten off leaving a long tail for sewing.

FINISHING

Lighty block squares to measurements.

Embroidery

Refer to photo. Using a single strand of black, embroider

eyes and nose in satin stitch, center of lip in straight stitch and muzzle outlines in open lazy-daisy stitch. Sew on ears.

Left side border

Position a square so LH edge is at top. From RS, join C with a sl st in side edge of last row, ch 2.

Row 1 Work 1 hdc in each row to bottom edge—24 sts. Ch 2, turn.

Rows 2–5 Hdc in each st across. Ch 2, turn. After row 5 is completed, do not ch, fasten off. Work border on 5 more squares. Place 2 squares with borders side by side, then place a plain square on the left. Sew side edge of these squares tog forming a strip. Rep twice more.

Horizontal border

From RS, join C with a sl st in top RH edge of one strip.

Row 1 Work 1 hdc in each st across entire top edge—94 sts. Ch 2, turn.

Rows 2–5 Hdc in each st across. Ch 2, turn. After row 5 is completed, do not ch, fasten off. Rep once more. Place one strip with border above another strip with border, then place plain strip above them. Sew strips tog, as shown.

Outer border

From RS, join C with a sl st in center of any side edge.

Rnd 1 Ch 2, making sure that work lies flat, hdc evely around entire edge working 3 hdc in each corner. Join rnd with a sl st in first hdc.

Rnds 2–5 Ch 2, hdc in each st around, working 3 hdc in each corner st. Join rnd with a sl st in first hdc. After rnd 5 is completed, fasten off.

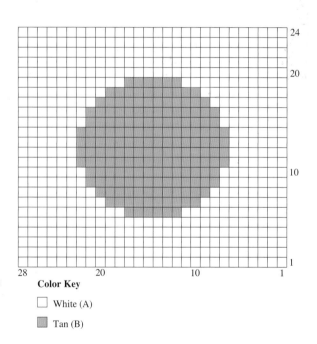

Color Key

☐ White (A)

▨ Tan (B)

Whip up a friendly feline throw your child will love. With crocheted ears and adorable embroidered whiskers, it will have your little one begging to curl up for a catnap.

purr-fection

FINISHED MEASURMENTS

• 35" x 35"/89 x 89cm

MATERIALS

• 5 1¾oz/50g balls (each approx 114yd/105m) of Wendy/Berroco, Inc.'s **Velvet Touch** (nylon) in #1209 pink (MC) ⓸

• 2 balls in #1200 white (CC)

• Sportweight yarn in medium blue, medium pink and tan for embroidery

• Size H/8 (5mm) crochet hook or size to obtain gauge

• Bobbins

• Yarn needle

• Pink sewing thread

• Sewing needle

GAUGES

• 12 sts and 10 rows to 4"/10cm over hdc using size H/8 (5mm) hook.

• One square 9½"/24cm using size H/8 (5mm) hook. Take time to check gauges.

NOTES

1 See page 194 for how to work color changes.

2 Wind CC onto two separate bobbins and MC onto one bobbin.

SQUARE

(make 9)

With CC, ch 30.

Row 1 (WS) Hdc in 3rd ch from hook and in each ch across—28 sts. Ch 2, turn.

Rows 2–5 Hdc in each st across. Ch 2, turn.

Beg chart

Row 6 (RS) Beg at st 1 and work to st 28. Work as established until row 24 is completed. Fasten off.

EARS

(make 18)

With MC, ch 2.

Row 1 In 2nd ch from hook, work (sc, 2 hdc, dc, 2 hdc, sc). Ch 1, turn.

Row 2 Sc in first st, work 2 hdc in next st, 2 dc in next st, tr in next st, 2 dc in next st, 2 hdc in next st, sc in last st. Fasten off leaving a long tail for sewing onto blanket.

FINISHING

Lighty block squares to measurements.

Embroidery

Refer to photo and use a single strand of yarn in needle. Working in satin stitch, embroider eyes using medium blue and nose using medium pink. Using medium pink, embroider center of lip in straight stitch and cheek outlines in open lazy-daisy stitch. Using tan, embroider whiskers in straight stitch.

Ears

Using pink thread and sewing needle, pinch top of ear tog to form a point; sew point to secure. Sew on ears as shown.

Left side border

Position a square so LH edge is at top. From RS, join MC with a sl in side edge of last row, ch 2.

Row 1 Work 1 hdc in each row to bottom edge—24 sts. Ch 2, turn.

Rows 2–5 Hdc in each st across. Ch 2, turn. After row 5 is completed, do not ch, fasten off. Work border on 5 more squares. Place 2 squares with borders side by side, then place a plain square on the left. Sew side edge of these squares tog forming a strip. Rep twice more.

Horizontal border

From RS, join MC with a sl st in top RH edge of one strip.

Row 1 Work 1 hdc in each st across entire top edge—94 sts. Ch 2, turn.

Rows 2–5 Hdc in each st across. Ch 2, turn. After row 5 is completed, do not ch, fasten off. Rep once more. Place one strip with border above another strip with border, then place plain strip above them. Sew strips tog, as shown.

Outer border

From RS, join MC with a sl st in center of any side edge.

Rnd 1 Ch 2, making sure that work lies flat, hdc evenly around entire edge working 3 hdc in each corner. Join rnd with a sl st in first hdc.

Rnds 2–5 Ch 2, hdc in each st around, working 3 hdc in each corner st. Join rnd with a sl st in first hdc. After rnd 5 is completed, fasten off.

Color Key

☐ White (CC)

☐ Pink (MC)

Crocheted in one piece, this woolly wonder will keep your little lamb warm all night long. The sheep are crocheted separately and sewn on, adding depth and dimension to this eye-catching blanket.

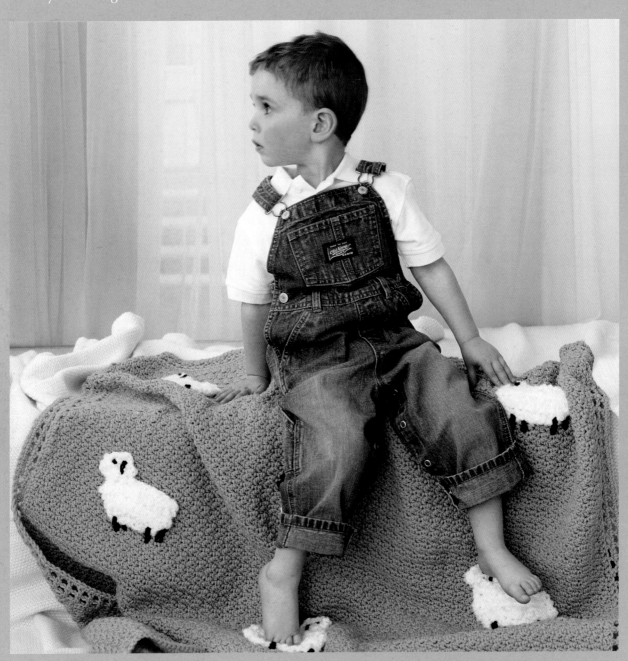

farm fresh

FINISHED MEASUREMENTS

• 36" x 38"/91.5 x 96.5cm (not including border)

MATERIALS

• 5 5oz/143g balls (each approx 290yd/265m) of Red Heart/Coats & Clark's **Kids** (acrylic) in #2652 lime (MC) [4]

• 1 6oz/170g ball (each approx 140yd/128m) of Red Heart/Coats & Clark's **Light & Lofty** (acrylic) each in #9311 cloud (A) and #9312 onyx (B) [6]

• Worsted weight yarn in white and black for embroidery

• Size H/8 and K/10½ (5 and 7mm) crochet hooks or sizes to obtain gauge

• Yarn needle

NOTE

One of the original colors used in this project is no longer available. The following substitution is recommended:

• **Light & Lofty** #9316 puff for **Light & Lofty** #9311 cloud (A)

GAUGES

• 12 sts and 10 rows to 4"/10cm over pat st using MC and size H/8 (5mm) hook.

• 10 sts and 8 rows to 4"/10cm over sc using A and size K/10½ (7mm) hook.

Take time to check gauges.

BLANKET

With H/8 (5mm) hook and MC, ch 109. **Row 1** Sc in 2nd ch from hook, dc in next ch, * sc in next ch, dc in next ch; rep from * across—108 sts. Ch 1, turn. **Row 2** *Sc in next st, dc in next st; rep from * across. Ch 1, turn. Rep row 2 for pat st and work until piece measures 38"/96.5cm from beg. Fasten off.

SHEEP

(make 8)

With K/10½ (7mm) hook and A, ch 9. **Row 1** Sc in 2nd ch from hook and in each ch across—8 sts. Ch 1, turn. **Row 2** Work 2 sc in first st, sc in next 6 sts, work 2 sc in last st—10 sts. Ch 1, turn. **Row 3** Work 2 sc in first st, sc in next 8 sts, work 2 sc in last st—12 sts. Ch 1, turn. **Row 4** Sc in first 8 sts, [dec 1 st over next 2 sts] twice—10 sts. Ch 1, turn. **Row 5** Dec 1 st over first 2 sts, sc in next st, hdc in next st, sc in next 2 sts, sl st in next st, sc in next 2 sts, do not work last st—8 sts. Ch 1, turn. **Row 6** Work 2 sc in first st, sc in next st—3 sts. Ch 1, turn. **Row 7** Sc in first 2 sts, work 3 sc in last st—5 sts. Ch 1, turn. **Row 8** Dec 1 st over first 2 sts, hdc in next st, dec 1 st over last 2 sts—3 sts. Fasten off. Make 6 more sheep using A and 1 using B.

FINISHING

Lightly block blanket to measurements. Referring to photo, sew on sheep.

Embroidery

For white sheep, use black worsted weight yarn. Make French knot eyes, and chain stitch ears and legs, as shown. For black sheep, use white worsted weight yarn and work as for white sheep.

Fence border

From RS with H/8 (5mm) hook, join MC with a sl st in first st or row after any corner.

Rnd 1 Ch 1, making sure that work lies flat, sc evenly around entire edge, working 3 sc in each corner. Join rnd with a sl st in first sc.

Rnd 2 Ch 3, *ch 1, sk next st, dc in next st; rep from * around, working (dc, ch 1, dc, ch 1, dc) in center sc of each corner. Join rnd with a sl st in 3rd ch of ch-3.

Rnd 3 Ch 3, *ch 1, sk next ch-1 sp, dc in next dc; rep from * around, working (dc, ch 1, dc, ch 1, dc) in center dc of each corner. Join rnd with a sl st in 3rd ch of ch-3.

Rnd 4 Ch 1, sc in same st as joining, sc in each dc and ch-1 sp around, working 3 sc in center dc of each corner. Join rnd with a sl st in first sc. Fasten off.

*Q*uick stripes and easy patchwork squares work together in perfect harmony in this comely design. Crochet the stripe and gingham blocks individually, join them together, and then finish the look with a clean single crochet stitch border.

square dance

FINISHED MEASUREMENTS

• 31½" x 32¼"/80 x 82cm (not including border)

MATERIALS

• 4 1¾oz/50g balls (each approx 123yd/113m) of Rowan Yarns/Westminster Fibers' **Wool Cotton** (wool/cotton) in #901 citron (A), #900 antique (B) and #946 elf (C) ⓷

• 3 balls in #953 august (D)

• Size H/8 (5mm) crochet hook or size to obtain gauge

• Bobbins

• Yarn needle

NOTE

One of the original yarns used in this project is no longer available. The following substitution is recommended:

• #909 french navy for #953 august (D)

GAUGES

• 16 sts and 20 rows to 4"/10cm over sc using size H/8 (5mm) hook.

• One block to 10½" x 10¾"/26.5 x 27.5cm using size H/8 (5mm) hook.

Take time to check gauges.

NOTES

1 See page 194 for how to work color changes.

2 When working gingham blocks, wind A and C onto two separate bobbins each and B onto one bobbin.

STRIPE BLOCK

(make 4)

With A, ch 43.

Row 1 Sc in 2nd ch from hook and in each ch across—42 sts. Ch 1, turn.

Row 2 Sc in each st across. Join D, ch 1, turn. Rep row 2 for pat st and cont in stripe pat as foll: *work 2 rows each in D, B, C and A; rep from * until a total of 54 rows have been completed. Fasten off.

GINGHAM BLOCK

(make 5)

With A, ch 43.

Row 1 Sc in 2nd ch from hook and in next 13 ch, change to B, sc in next 14 ch, change to A, sc in last 14 ch—42 sts. Ch 1, turn.

Row 2 With A, sc in first 14 sts, with B, sc in next 14 sts, with A, sc in last 14 sts. Ch 1, turn.

Rows 3–18 Rep row 2. When row 18 is completed, change to C, ch 1, turn.

Rows 19–36 With C, sc in first 14 sts, with A, sc in next 14 sts, with C, sc in last 14 sts. Ch 1, turn. When row 36 is completed, change to A, ch 1, turn.

Rows 37–54 Rep row 2. When row 54 is completed, do not ch, fasten off.

FINISHING

Lightly block pieces to measurements.

Embroidery

Use D doubled in needle throughout and make sure to maintain st and row gauge when weaving. For horizontal stitching lines, weave under and over every st between rows 9 and 10, 27 and 28, and 44 and 45. For vertical stitching lines, weave under and over every row between sts 7 and 8, 21 and 22, and 35 and 36. Referring to photo, sew blocks tog.

Border

From RS, join D with a sl st in any corner.

Rnd 1 Ch 1, making sure that work lies flat, sc evenly around, working 3 sc in each corner. Join rnd with a sl st in first sc.

Rnds 2–6 Ch 1, sc in each st around, working 3 sc in each corner st. Join rnd with a sl st in first sc. Fasten off.

A sumptuous oh-so-cuddly blanket makes the ultimate statement in luxury. Composed of squares and triangles, this easy-to-crochet number works up in no time, leaving you more time to curl up with your tot.

tickled pink

FINISHED MEASUREMENTS

- 36" x 36"/91.5 x 91.5cm (not including border)

MATERIALS

ORIGINAL YARN

- 5 1¾oz/50g balls (approx 137yd/125m) of Lion Brand Yarn's **Polarspun** (polyester) each in #101 polar pink (A) and #157 polar yellow (B)
- 1 ball in #100 snow white (C)

SUBSTITUTE YARN

- 9 1¾oz/50g balls (each approx 90yd/83m) of Berroco Inc.'s **Berroco Plush** (nylon) each in #1947 bubblegum (A) and #1928 birdy (B)
- 1 ball in #1901 crema (C)
- Size H/8 (5mm) crochet hook or size to obtain gauge
- Yarn needle

GAUGE

One square to 12"/30.5cm using size H/8 (5mm) hook.

Take time to check gauge.

SQUARE

(make 5)

With A, ch 4 loosely. Join ch with a sl st forming a ring.

Rnd 1 (WS) Ch 2 (counts as 1 hdc), work 2 hdc in ring, [ch 2 for corner sp, 3 hdc in ring] 3 times, end ch 2 for last corner sp. Join rnd with a sl st in 2nd ch of ch-2. Turn.

Rnd 2 (RS) Ch 3 (counts as 1 dc), [work (2 dc, ch 2, 2 dc) in corner ch-2 sp, dc in next 3 sts] 3 times, end work (2 dc, ch 2, 2 dc) in corner ch-2 sp, dc in last 2 sts—7 dc each side. Join rnd with a sl st in 3rd ch of ch-3. Turn.

Rnd 3 Ch 2 (counts as 1 hdc), hdc in next 5 sts, [work (2 hdc, ch 2, 2 hdc) in corner ch-2 sp, hdc in next 7 sts] 3 times, end work (2 hdc, ch 2, 2 hdc) in corner ch-2 sp, hdc in last st—11 hdc each side. Join rnd with a sl st in 2nd ch of ch-2. Turn.

Rnd 4 Ch 3 (counts as 1 dc), dc in next 2 sts, [work (2 dc, ch 2, 2 dc) in corner ch-2 sp, dc in next 11 sts] 3 times, end work (2 dc, ch 2, 2 dc) in corner ch-2 sp, dc in last 8 sts—15 dc each side. Join rnd with a sl st in 3rd ch of ch-3. Turn.

Rnd 5 Ch 2 (counts as 1 hdc), hdc in next 10 sts, [work (2 hdc, ch 2, 2 hdc) in corner ch-2 sp, hdc in next 15 sts] 3 times, end work (2 hdc, ch 2, 2 hdc) in corner ch-2 sp, hdc in last 4 sts—19 hdc each side. Join rnd with a sl st in 2nd ch of ch-2. Turn.

Rnd 6 Ch 3 (counts as 1 dc), dc in each st to corner, [work (2 dc, ch 2, 2 dc) in corner ch-2 sp, dc in each st to corner] 3 times, end work (2 dc, ch 2, 2 dc) in corner ch-2 sp, dc in each st to beg—23 dc each side. Join rnd with a sl st in 3rd ch of ch-3. Turn.

Rnd 7 Ch 2 (counts as 1 hdc), hdc in each st to corner, [work (2 hdc, ch 2, 2 hdc) in corner ch-2 sp, hdc in each st to corner] 3 times, end work (2 hdc, ch 2, 2 hdc) in corner ch-2 sp, hdc in each st to beg—27 hdc each side. Join rnd with a sl st in 2nd ch of ch-2. Turn. Cont to rep rows 6 and 7 (having 4 additional sts on each side every rnd) until square measures 12"/30.5cm. Fasten off. Make 3 more using A and make 1 using B.

SIDE HALF-SQUARE

(make 4)

With B, ch 4 loosely. Join ch with a sl st forming a ring.

Row 1 (WS) Ch 3 loosely (counts as 1 hdc and ch 1), work 2 hdc in ring, ch 2 for corner sp, work 2 hdc in ring, ch 1, hdc in ring for side sp. Turn.

Row 2 (RS) Ch 4 loosely (counts as 1 dc and ch 1), work 2 dc in ch-1 sp, dc in each st to corner sp, work (2 dc, ch 2, 2 dc) in corner ch-2 sp, dc in each st to ch-1 sp, work 2 dc in ch-1 sp, end ch 1, dc in 2nd ch of ch-3 of previous row—-7 dc each side. Turn.

Row 3 Ch 3 loosely (counts as 1 hdc and ch 1), work 2 hdc in ch-1 sp, hdc in each st to ch-2 sp, work (2 hdc, ch 2, 2 hdc) in corner ch-2 sp, hdc in each st to ch-1 sp, work 2 hdc in ch-1 sp, end ch 1, hdc in 3rd ch of ch-4 of previous row—-11 hdc each side. Turn. Cont to rep rows 2 and 3 (having 4 additional sts on each

side every row) until sides of triangle measure 12"/30.5cm. Fasten off. Make 3 more using B.

CORNER HALF-SQUARE

(make 4)

Work as for side half-square until base of triangle measures 12"/30.5cm across.

FINISHING

Lightly block pieces to measurements. Referring to photo, whipstitch pieces tog as shown.

Blanket embroidery

Take care to maintain st and row gauge when working chain-stitches. Referring to photo, use C to embroider diagonal chain stitch lines; as shown.

Border

From RS, join A with a sl st in center of any side edge.

Rnd 1 Ch 1, making sure that work lies flat, sc evenly around entire edge, working 3 sc in each corner. Join rnd with a sl st in first sc. Turn. **Rnds 2–4** Ch 2, hdc in each st around, working 3 hdc in center st of each corner. Join rnd with a sl st on first hdc. Turn. When rnd 4 is completed, join rnd with a sl st on first hdc, fasten off.

Border embroidery

Take care to maintain st and row gauge when working chain stitches. Referring to photo, use C to embroider a line of chain stitches along rnd 2, as shown.

W rap your baby in tradition with this argyle throw. Crocheted in snuggly soft cotton, this blanket is made in individual strips, then sewn together and accented with a chain stitch and complementary border.

english beat

• 31" x 34½"/78.5 x 87.5cm (not including border)

MATERIALS

• 3 3½oz/100g balls (each approx 205yd/187m) of *Classic Elite Yarns'* **Provence** *(mercerized cotton) each in #2612 yellow (A) and #2647 delft blue (B)* **3**
• *1 ball in #2608 light blue (C)*
• *Size H/8 (5mm) crochet hook or size to obtain gauge*
• *Bobbins*
• *Yarn needle*

NOTE

Two of the original colors used for this blanket are no longer available. The following substitutions are recommended:
• *#2650 new moon for #2612 yellow (A)*
• *#2646 island blue for #2608 light blue (C)*

GAUGE

14 sts and 10 rows to 4"/10cm over hdc using size H/8 (5mm) hook.
Take time to check gauge.

NOTES

1 Blanket is made in three strips.
2 See page 194 for how to work color changes.
3 Wind A onto two separate bobbins.

With A, ch 41.

Row 1 (RS) Hdc in 3rd ch from hook and in each ch across—39 sts. Ch 2, turn.

Row 2 Hdc in each st across. Ch 2, turn. Rep row 2 for pat st.

Beg chart

Row 3 (RS) Beg at st 1 and work to st 39. Cont to work as established to row 78. Fasten off.

STRIP 2

Work as for strip 1 and 2, but working rows 3-39 using C instead of B and rows 40–76 using B instead of C.

FINISHING

Lightly block strips to measurements. Referring to photo, sew strips tog as shown.

Embroidery

Take care to maintain st and row gauge when working chain stitches. Referring to photo, use C to embroider diagonal lines of chain stitches across B diamonds and B to embroider diagonal lines of chain stitches across C diamonds, as shown.

Border

From RS, join A with a sl st in center of any side edge.

Rnd 1 Ch 2, making sure that work lies flat, hdc evenly around entire edge, working 3 hdc in each corner. Join rnd with a sl st in first hdc. Fasten off. From RS, join B with a sl st in center st of any side edge.

Rnd 2 Ch 1, sc in same st as joining, *ch 1, sk next st, sc in next st; rep from * around, working (sc, ch 3, sc) in each corner st. Join rnd with a sl st in ch-1. Sl st in next ch-1 sp, turn.

Rnd 3 (WS) Ch 2, hdc in same st as sl st, work 2 hdc in each ch-1 sp around, working (2 hdc, ch 2, 2 hdc) in each corner ch-3 sp. Join rnd with a sl st in 2nd ch of ch-2. Ch 1, turn.

Rnd 4 Working through back lps, sc in next st, *ch 1, sk next st, sc in next st; rep from * around, working (sc, ch 3, sc) in each corner ch-2 sp. Join rnd with a sl st in first sc. Sl st to next ch-1 sp, turn.

Rnd 5 (WS) Rep rnd 3. Join rnd with a sl st in 2nd ch of ch-2.

Rnd 6 (WS) Ch 1, working through front lps, sc in each st around, working (2 sc, ch 2, 2 sc) in each corner ch-2 sp. Join rnd with a sl st in first sc. Fasten off.

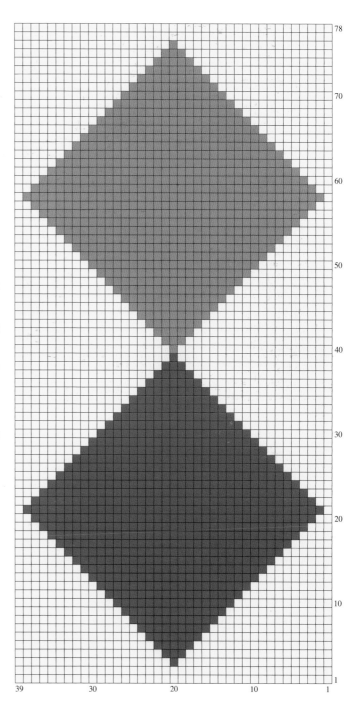

Color Key

☐ Yellow (A)

■ Delft blue (B)

■ Lt blue (C)

et ready to make some waves with this jewel-toned treasure that's sure to please
your little gem. A carefree chevron pattern worked in vibrant berry hues is accented with
whimsical pompoms.

ripple effect

FINISHED MEASUREMENTS

• 36" x 36"/91.5 x 91.5cm

MATERIALS

ORIGINAL YARN

• 2 1¾oz/50g balls (each approx 130yd/119m) of Jaeger Handknits/Westminster Fibers' **Matchmaker Merino DK** (wool) in #887 fuchsia (A), #883 petal (B), #888 parma (C), #882 haze (D), #870 rosy (E), #881 trellis (F) and #876 clarice (G) ③

SUBSTITUTE YARN

• 2 1¾oz/50g balls (each approx 148yd/135m) of Schulana/Skacel Collection Inc.'s **Merino Cotton 135** (cotton/wool) each in #13 fuchsia (A), #3 pink (B), #32 purple (C), #4 light blue (D), #9 orange (E), #31 apricot (F) and #21 red (G) ③

• Size H/8 (5mm) crochet hook or size to obtain gauge

GAUGE

20 sts and 11 rows to 4"/10cm over pat st using size H/8 (5mm) hook.

Take time to check gauge.

NOTE

See page 194 for how to work color changes.

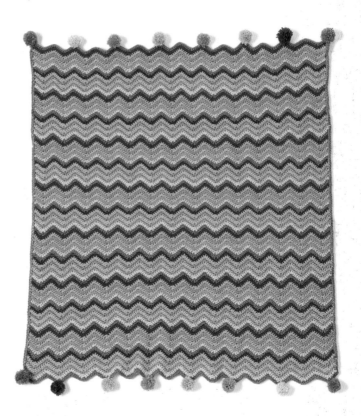

BLANKET

With A, ch 183.

Row 1 Work 2 hdc in 3rd ch from hook, hdc in next 4 ch, * sk next 2 ch, hdc in next 5 ch, work 3 hdc in next ch, hdc in next 5 ch; rep from *, end sk next 2 ch, hdc in next 4 ch, work 2 hdc in last ch—181 sts. Join B, ch 2, turn.

Row 2 Work 2 hdc in first st, hdc in next 4 sts, * sk next 2 sts, hdc in next 5 sts, work 3 hdc in next st, hdc in next 5 sts; rep from *, end sk next 2 sts, hdc in next 4 sts, work 2 hdc in last st. Join C, ch 2, turn. Rep row 2 for pat st and work in stripe pat as foll: 1 row each C, D, E, F, G, A and B. Work even until piece measures approx 36"/91.5cm, end with 1 row A.

FINISHING

Lightly block piece to measurements.

Edging

From RS with A, join yarn with a sl st in side edge of first row. Making sure that work lies flat, sc evenly along side edge to last row. Fasten off. Rep along opposite side edge.

Pompoms

Make 1½"/4cm in diameter pompoms as foll: 4 using A and 2 each using B, C, D, E, F and G. Referring to photo, sew pompoms to points as shown.

For your child's safety, please ensure that pompoms are sewn securely to blanket.

Nap time never felt this good! Crocheted separately and then stitched together, cheerful blocks in ocean hues come together in this cradle-friendly throw. An ivory border and embroidered accents throughout make for striking contrasts.

blue marine

FINISHED MEASUREMENTS

• 30" x 30"/76 x 76cm (not including edging)

MATERIALS

• 6 1¾ oz/50g balls (each approx 108yd/99m) of Tahki Yarns/Tahki•Stacy Charles, Inc.'s **Cotton Classic** (mercerized cotton) in #3815 lt. aqua (A) and 3804 teal (B) **4**

• 2 balls in #3003 off white (C)

• 1 ball in #3786 dark teal (D)

• Size H/8 (5mm) crochet hook or size to obtain gauge

• Yarn needle

GAUGES

• 14 sts and 12 rows to 4"/10cm over hdc using size H/8 (5mm) hook.

• One square to 6"/15cm using size H/8 (5mm) hook. Take time to check gauges.

SQUARE

(make 25)

With A, ch 24.

Row 1 Hdc in 3rd ch from hook and in each ch across—22 sts. Ch 2, turn.

Row 2 Hdc in each st across. Ch 2, turn. Rep row 2 for pat st and work until a total of 18 rows have been completed. Fasten off. Make 11 more using A, 9 using B and 4 using C.

FINISHING

Lightly block squares to measurements. Referring to photo, sew squares tog.

Embroidery

Refer to photo. Use yarn doubled in needle throughout and make sure to maintain st and row gauge when weaving. Weave under and over every st or row. For horizontal stitching lines, beg at one side edge and end at opposite side edge. Weave C through center row of first, 3rd and 5th rows of squares, then weave D through center row of 2nd and 4th rows of squares; as shown. For vertical stitching lines, beg at bottom edge and end at top edge. Weave C between sts 11 and 12 of squares 1, 3 and 5, then weave D between sts 11 and 12 of squares 2 and 4, as shown.

Edging

From RS, join C with a sl st in center of any side edge.

Rnd 1 Ch 1, making sure that work lies flat, sc evenly around, working 3 sc in each corner. Join rnd with a sl st in first sc.

Rnd 2 Ch 3 (counts as 1 dc), turn. Dc in each st around, working 3 dc in each corner. Join rnd with a sl st in 3rd ch of ch-3. Fasten off.

All newborns deserve a handmade blanket stitched with love. A winsome combination of checkered blocks in ivory and plum hues, handsome plaid stitching and pretty scalloped edges gives plenty of vintage charm to this classic heirloom treasure.

peewee pizzazz

FINISHED MEASUREMENTS

• 39" x 37½"/99 x 95cm (not including border)

MATERIALS

• 5 6oz/172g balls (each approx 312yd/285m) of TLC/Coats & Clark's **Essentials** (acrylic) in #2316 winter white (MC) 🔲4

• 2 balls in #2531 light plum (A)

• 1 ball each in #2533 dark plum (B) and #2672 light thyme (C)

• Size H/8 (5mm) crochet hook or size to obtain gauge

• Bobbins

• Yarn needle

GAUGES

• 18 sts to 5"/12.5cm and 10 rows to 4"/10cm over pat st using size H/8 (5mm) hook.

• One block to 13" x 12½"/33 x 31.5cm using size H/8 (5mm) hook.

Take time to check gauges.

NOTES

1 See page 194 for how to work color changes.

2 Wind MC onto one bobbin, and A and B onto two separate bobbins each.

SOLID BLOCK

(make 4)

With MC, ch 48.

Row 1 Sc in 2nd ch from hook, *sk next ch, work 3 sc in next ch, sk next ch; rep from *, end sc in last ch—47 sts. Ch 1, turn.

Row 2 Sc in first st, *sk next st, work 3 sc in next st, sk next st; rep from *, end sc in last st. Ch 1, turn. Rep row 2 for pat st and work until a total of 32 rows have been completed. When row 32 is completed, do not ch, fasten off.

GINGHAM BLOCK

(make 5)

With A, ch 48.

Row 1 Sc in 2nd ch from hook [sk next ch, work 3 sc in next ch, sk next ch] 5 times changing to MC, [sk next ch, work 3 sc in next ch, sk next ch] 5 times changing to A, [sk next ch, work 3 sc in next ch, sk next ch] 5 times, end sc in last ch—47 sts. Ch 1, turn.

Rows 2–10 Sc in first st, [sk next st, work 3 sc in next st, sk next st] 5 times changing to MC, [sk next st, work 3 sc in next st, sk next st] 5 times changing to A, [sk next st, work 3 sc in next st, sk next st] 5 times, end sc in last st. Ch 1, turn. When row 10 is completed, join B, ch 1, turn.

Rows 11–21 Sc in first st, [sk next st, work 3 sc in next st, sk next st] 5 times changing to A, [sk next st, work 3 sc in next st, sk next st] 5 times changing to B, [sk next st, work 3 sc in next st, sk next st] 5 times, end sc in last st. Ch 1, turn. When row 21 is completed, join A, ch 1, turn.

Rows 22–31 Rep row 2. When row 31 is completed, work with A only, ch 1, turn.

Row 32 Sc in first st, *sk next st, work 3 sc in next st, sk next st; rep from *, end sc in last st. Fasten off.

FINISHING

Lightly block squares to measurements. Referring to photo, sew blocks tog as shown.

Embroidery

Use a single strand of C in needle throughout and make sure to maintain st and row gauge when weaving. For horizontal stitching lines, work from one side edge to the opposite side edge. Weave under and over every st along centers of each gingham block, as shown. For vertical stitching lines, work from bottom edge to top edge. Weave under and over every row along centers of each gingham block, as shown.

Border

From RS, join MC with a sl st in any corner.

Rnd 1 Ch 1, sc in same st as joining, *work 102 sc evenly spaced across edge to corner, work 3 sc in corner; rep from * around, end last rep with 2 sc in beg corner. Join rnd with a sl st in first sc.

Rnd 2 Sl st in sc, ** *sc in next st, ch 4, sk next 2 sts; rep from * to 1 st before corner, sc in next st, ch 3, sk 3 corner sts, sc in next sc; rep from ** around—34 ch-4 sps each side. Join rnd with a sl st in first sc.

Rnd 3 Sl st to center of ch 4, ** *sc in next ch 4-sp, ch 4; rep from * to corner ch-3 sp, work (sc, ch 3, sc) in corner sp; rep from ** around—35 ch-4 sps each side. Join rnd with a sl st.

Rnd 4 Sl st to center of first ch-4 sp, ch 1, sc in same sp, ** *work (3 dc, ch 2, 3 dc) in next ch-4 sp, sc in next ch-4 sp; rep from * to corner ch-3 sp, work (4 dc, ch 3, 4 dc) in corner sp; rep from ** around—17 points each side. Join rnd with a sl st in ch-1. Fasten off, turn.

Rnd 5 From WS, join C with a sl st in center ch of any corner ch-3 sp. Working through front lps only and making sure that work lies flat, sl st in each st and ch around. Join rnd with a sl st in first sl st. Fasten off.

This delightful afghan is sure to be a favorite for any child and an instant heirloom to pass along to future generations. Bold colors, punchy patchwork and easy stitching work together in a striking combination. A decorative border makes a quick finish to the entire design.

pattern play

FINISHED MEASUREMENTS

• 23" x 36"/58.5 x 91.5cm (not including border)

MATERIALS

• 4 1¾oz/50g balls (each approx 123yd/113m) of Rowan Yarns/Westminster Fibers' **Wool Cotton** (wool/cotton) in #901citron (A), #900 antique (B) and #946 elf (C)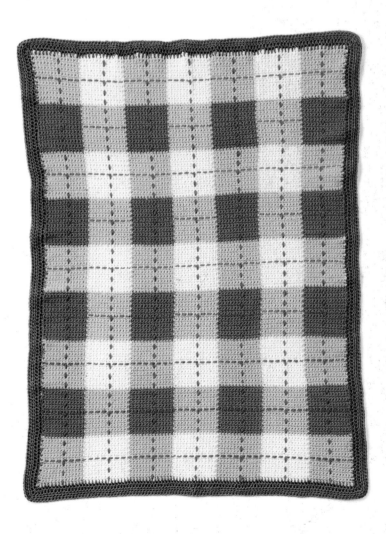
• 3 balls in #953 august (D)
• Size G/7 (4.5mm) crochet hook or size to obtain gauge
• Bobbins
• Yarn needle

NOTE

One of the original colors used in this project is no longer available. The following substitution is recommended:

• #909 french navy for #953 august (D)

GAUGE

17 sts and 20 rows to 4"/10cm over sc and gingham pat using size G/6 (4.5mm) hook.
Take time to check gauge.

NOTES

1 Blanket is made in one piece.
2 See page 194 for how to work color changes.
3 When working gingham pat, wind A and C onto four separate bobbins each, and B onto three separate bobbins.

BLANKET

With A, ch 99.

Foundation row Sc in 2nd ch from hook and in each ch across—98 sts. Ch 1, turn

Gingham Pattern

Rows 1–20 *With A, sc in next 14 sts, with B, sc in next 14 sts; rep from *, end with A, sc in last 14 sts. Ch 1, turn. After row 20 has been completed, join C, ch 1, turn.

Rows 21–40 *With C, sc in next 14 sts, with A, sc in next 14 sts; rep from *, end with C, sc in last 14 sts. Ch 1, turn. After row 40 has been completed, join A, ch 1, turn.

Rows 41–60 Rep rows 1–20.

Rows 61–80 Rep rows 21–40.

Rows 81–100 Rep rows 1–20.

Rows 101–120 Rep rows 21–40.

Rows 121–140 Rep rows 1–20.

Rows 141–160 Rep rows 21–40.

Rows 161–180 Rep rows 1–20. After row 180 is completed, do not ch, fasten off.

FINISHING

Lightly block piece to measurements.

Embroidery

Use D doubled in needle throughout and make sure to maintain st and row gauge when weaving. For horizontal stitching lines, weave under and over every st between rows 10 and 11, and 30 and 31 to top. For vertical stitching lines, weave under and over every 2 rows between sts 7 and 8, 21 and 22 across, then cont across as shown.

Border

From RS, join D with a sl st in any corner.

Rnd 1 Ch 2, making sure that work lies flat, hdc evenly around, working 3 hdc in each corner. Join rnd with a sl st in first hdc.

Rnds 2–3 Ch 2, hdc in each st around, working 3 hdc in each corner st. Join rnd with a sl st in first hdc. Fasten off.

Easy as 1-2-3, this rich serape-style throw is a cinch to crochet. Inspired by the sunsets of the Southwest, it's worked in eye-popping colors and makes a luminous addition to almost any nursery.

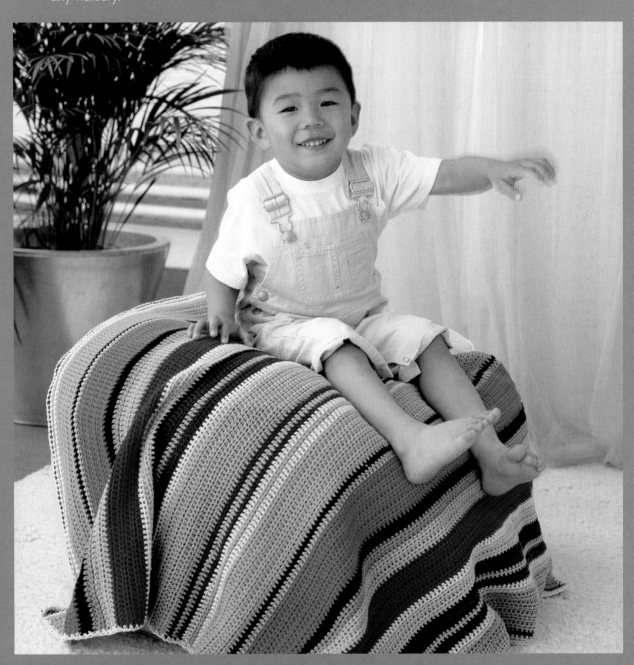

navajo throw

FINISHED MEASUREMENTS

- 34" x 36"/86 x 91.5cm

MATERIALS

- 2 1¾oz/50g balls (each approx 108yd/99m) of Tahki Yarns/Tahki•Stacy Charles, Inc.'s **Cotton Classic** (mercerized cotton) in #3873 royal blue (A), #3805 aqua (C), #3450 fuchsia (F), #3841 light blue (I) and #3715 chartreuse (J) 〔4〕
- 1 ball each in #3003 off white (B), #3002 black (D), #3351 coral (E), #3936 lavender (G) and #3995 wine (H)
- Size H/8 (5mm) crochet hook or size to obtain gauge

GAUGE

15 sts and 13 rows to 4"/10cm over hdc using size H/8 (5mm) hook.

Take time to check gauge.

NOTES

See page 194 for how to work color changes.

BLANKET

With A, ch 130.

Row 1 Hdc in 3rd ch from hook and in each ch across—128 sts. Join B, ch 2, turn.

Row 2 Hdc in each st across. Join C, ch 2, turn. Rep row 2 for pat st and work in stripe pat.

Stripe Pattern

* Work 1 row C, 1 row B, 8 rows C, 1 row D, 1 row E, 8 rows F, 2 rows D, 2 rows G, 3 rows E, 6 rows H, 1 row B, 3 rows I, 1 row D, 2 rows A, 1 row E, 2 rows A, 1 row B, 1 row I, 8 rows J, 1 row A and 1 row I *, end 1 row A and 1 row B. Rep between * once more. Fasten off.

FINISHING

Lightly block piece to measurements.

Edging

From RS, join B with a sl st in any corner, ch 1. Rnd 1 Making sure that work lies flat, sc evenly around entire edge, working 3 sc in each corner. Join rnd with a sl st in ch-1. Fasten off.

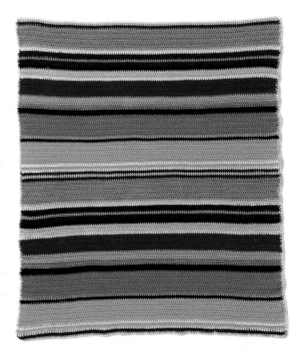

Add some texture to your little one's dreams with this fetching blanket. Treble-crochet diamonds bring the rich color to life. Baby will love its soft cozy feel, and you'll love its simple pattern stitch repeat!

true blue

FINISHED MEASUREMENTS

• 33" x 36½"/84 x 92.5cm (not including border)

MATERIALS

ORIGINAL YARN

• 5 5oz/143g balls (each approx 290yd/265m) of Red Heart/Coats & Clark's **Kids** (acrylic) in #2652 periwinkle (MC) **4**

• 1 3oz/85g ball (each approx 192yd/175m) of Red Heart/Coats & Clark's **Baby Teri** (acrylic/nylon) in #9101 white (CC) **4**

SUBSTITUTE YARN

• 8 3½oz/100g balls (each approx 190yd/174m) of Red Heart/Coats & Clark's **Classic** (acrylic) in #827 light periwinkle (MC) **4**

• 1 ball of Red Heart/Coats & Clark's **Baby Teri** in

#9101 white (CC) **4** (same as original)

• Size H/8 (5mm) crochet hook or size to obtain gauge

GAUGE

16 sts to 5"/12.5cm and 14 rows to 4"/10cm over diamond bobble pat using size H/8 (5mm) hook. Take time to check gauge.

NOTES

1 Blanket is made vertically.

2 Push all tr sts to RS as you work.

BLANKET

With CC, ch 119.

Foundation row 1 (WS) Hdc in 3rd ch from hook and each ch across—117 sts. Ch 1, turn.

Foundation row 2 Working though back lps only, sc in each st across. Fasten off, do not turn.

Diamond bobble pattern

Row 1 (RS) From RS, join MC with a sl st in first st at RH edge. Ch 3, dc in each st across. Ch 1, turn.

Row 2 Working through front lps only, sc in each st across—117 sts. Ch 1, turn.

Row 3 Sc in first 2 sts, *sc in next 4 sts, tr in next st, sc in next 3 sts; rep from *, end sc in last 3 sts. Ch 1, turn.

Row 4 Sc in first 3 sts, *sc in next 2 sts, tr in next st, sc in next, tr in next st, sc in next 3 sts; rep from *, end sc in last 2 sts. Ch 1, turn.

Row 5 Sc in first 2 sts, *sc in next 2 sts, tr in next st, sc in next 3 sts, tr in next st, sc in next st; rep from * across, end sc in last 3 sts. Ch 1, turn.

Row 6 Sc in first 3 sts, *tr in next st, sc in next 5 sts, tr in next st, sc in next st; rep from * across, end sc in last 2 sts. Ch 1, turn.

Row 7 Sc in first 2 sts, *tr in next st, sc in next 3 sts, tr in next st, sc in 3 sts; rep from * across, end tr in next st, sc in last 2 sts. Ch 1, turn.

Row 8 Rep row 6.

Row 9 Rep row 5.

Row 10 Rep row 4.

Row 11 Rep row 3.

Row 12 Working through front lps only, dc in each st across. Fasten off, do not turn.

Row 13 From RS, join CC with a sl st in first st at RH edge. Ch 2, hdc in each st across. Ch 1, turn.

Row 14 Working through back lps only, sc in each st across. Fasten off, do not turn. Rep rows 1-14 six more times, end with row 14. Fasten off.

FINISHING

Lightly block piece to measurements.

Border

From RS, join MC with a sl st in center of any side edge.

Rnd 1 Ch 1, making sure that work lies flat, sc evenly around entire edge, working 3 sc in each corner. Join rnd with a sl st in first sc.

Rnd 2 Ch 3, working through back lps only, dc in each st around, working (2 dc, ch 1, 2 dc) in center st of each corner. Join rnd with a sl st in 3rd ch of ch-3.

Rnd 3 Ch 1, working through back lps only, sc in same sp as joining, sc in each st around, working 3 sc in each corner ch-1 sp. Join rnd with a sl st in first sc.

Rnd 4 Ch 1, working through back lps only, sc in same sp as joining, sc in each st around, working 3 sc in center st of each corner. Join rnd with a sl st in first sc.

Rnd 5 Working through front lps only and making sure that work lies flat, sl st each st around, working 3 sl sts in center st of each corner. Join rnd with a sl st in first sl st. Fasten off.

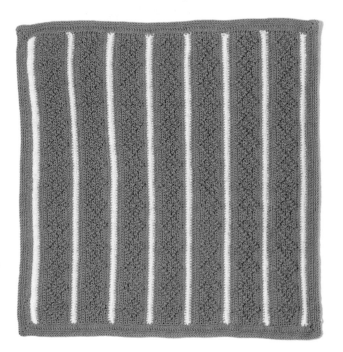

FOLLOWING CHARTS

Charts are a convenient way to follow colorwork patterns at a glance. When crocheting back and forth in rows, read charts from right to left on right side (RS) rows and from left to right on wrong side (WS) rows, repeating any stitch and row repeats as directed in the pattern. Posting a self-adhesive note under your working row is an easy way to keep track of your place.

COLORWORK CROCHETING

Two main types of colorwork are explored in this book: stripes and stranding.

Stripes

When working in single crochet, change color by drawing the new color through 2 loops on hook to complete the last single crochet, then working the next stitch with the new color, or, if at the end of the row, chain and turn.

For half double crochet, draw new color through 3 loops on hook to complete last half double crochet, work the next stitch with the new color, or, if at the end of the row, chain and turn.

When working in double crochet, draw

SLIP KNOT

1 Begin to crochet by making a slip knot. Make a loop several inches [or centimeters] from the end of the yarn. Insert the hook through the loop and catch the tail with the end.

2 Pull the yarn through the loop on the hook.

STANDARD YARN WEIGHT SYSTEM

Categories of yarn, gauge ranges and recommended needle and hook sizes

Yarn Weight Symbol & Category Names	**1** Super Fine	**2** Fine	**3** Light	**4** Medium	**5** Bulky	**6** Super Bulky
Type of Yarns in Category	Sock, Fingering, Baby	Sport, Baby	DK, Light Worsted	Worsted, Afghan, Aran	Chunky, Craft, Rug	Bulky, Roving
Knit Gauge Range* in Stockinette Stitch to 4 Inches	27–32 sts	23–26 sts	21–24 sts	16–20 sts	12–15 sts	6–11 sts
Recommended Needle in Metric Size Range	2.25–3.25 mm	3.25–3.75 mm	3.75–4.5 mm	4.5–5.5 mm	5.5–8 mm	8 mm and larger
Recommended Needle U.S. Size Range	1 to 3	3 to 5	5 to 7	7 to 9	9 to 11	11 and larger
Crochet Gauge* Ranges in Single Crochet To 4 Inch	21–32 sts	16–20 sts	12–17 sts	11–14 sts	8–11 sts	5–9 sts
Recommended Hook in Metric Size Range	2.25–3.5 mm	3.5–4.5 mm	4.5–5.5 mm	5.5–6.5 mm	6.5–9 mm	9 mm and larger
Recommended Hook U.S. Size Range	B–1 to E–4	E–4 to 7	7 to I–9	I–9 to K–10½	K–10½ to M–13	M–13 and larger

* GUIDELINES ONLY: The above reflect the most commonly used gauges and needle or hook sizes for specific yarn categories.

This *Standards & Guidelines* booklet and downloadable symbol artwork are available at: **YarnStandards.com**

CROCHET HOOKS

US	METRIC
14 steel	.60mm
12 steel	.75mm
10 steel	1.00mm
6 steel	1.50mm
5 steel	1.75mm
B/1	2.25mm
C/2	2.75mm
D/3	3.25mm
E/4	3.50mm
F/5	3.75mm
G/6	4.00mm
H/8	5.00mm
I/9	5.50mm
J/10	6.00mm
K/10.5	6.50mm
L/11	8.00mm

CHAIN

1 Pass yarn over the hook and catch it with the hook.

2 Draw yarn through the loop on the hook.

3 Repeat steps 1 and 2 to make a chain.

SINGLE CROCHET

1 Insert hook through top two loops of a stitch. Pass yarn over hook and draw up a loop—two loops on hook.

2 Pass yarn over hook and draw through both loops on hook.

3 Continue in the same way, inserting hook into each stitch.

HALF DOUBLE CROCHET

1 Pass yarn over hook. Insert hook through the top two loops of a stitch.

2 Pass yarn over hook and draw up a loop—three loops on hook. Pass yarn over hook.

3 Draw through all three loops on hook.

DOUBLE CROCHET

1 Pass yarn over hook. Insert hook through the top two loops of a stitch.

2 Pass yarn over hook and draw up a loop—three loops on hook.

3 Pass yarn over hook and draw it through the first two loops on the hook, pass yarn over hook and draw through the remaining two loops. Continue in the same way, inserting hook into each stitch.

new color through last 2 loops on hook to complete last double crochet, work the next stitch with the new color, or, if at the end of the row, chain and turn.

To prevent lumpy seams, do not make knots when changing colors. Instead, leave a long tail of yarn, then weave in tails after piece is completed and before sewing blocks together.

Intarsia

All the argyle designs are worked with separate bobbins of individual colors so there are no long strands of yarn. When changing color, pick up new color from under dropped color to prevent holes.

Stranding

When changing colors at the beginning of rows or rounds, carry yarn along for a few rows only, or cut yarn and rejoin when needed. It is important to keep the floats small and neat so they don't catch on small fingers when the garment is pulled on. When changing colors, pick up new color from under dropped color to prevent holes.

YARN SELECTION

For an exact reproduction of the projects photographed, use the yarn listed in the "Materials" section of the pattern. We've chosen yarns that are readily available in the U.S. and Canada at the time of printing. The Resources list on page 200 provides addresses of yarn distributors. Contact them for the name of a retailer in your area.

YARN SUBSTITUTION

You may wish to substitute yarns. Perhaps you

view small-scale projects as a chance to incorporate leftovers from your yarn stash, or the yarn specified may not be available in your area. You'll need to crochet to the given gauge to obtain the crocheted measurements with a substitute yarn (see "Gauge" on this page). Be sure to consider how the fiber content of the substitute yarn will affect the comfort and the ease of care of your projects.

To facilitate yarn substitution, yarns are graded by the standard stitch gauge obtained in single crochet. You'll find a grading number in the "Materials" section of the pattern, immediately following the fiber type of the yarn. Look for a substitute yarn that falls into the same category. The suggested hook size and gauge on the yarn label should be comparable to that on the "Standard Yarn Weight System" chart (see page 194).

After you've successfully gauge-swatched a substitute yarn, you'll need to figure out how much of the substitute yarn the project requires. First, find the total length of the original yarn in the pattern (multiply number of balls by yards/meters per ball). Divide this figure by the new yards/meters per ball (listed on the yarn label). Round up to the next whole number. The answer is the number of balls required.

GAUGE

It is always important to crochet a gauge swatch, and it is even more so with garments to ensure proper fit.

Patterns usually state gauge over a 4"/10cm span. However, it's beneficial to make a larger test swatch. This gives a more precise stitch gauge, a better idea of the appearance and drape of the crocheted fabric, and gives you a chance to familiarize yourself with the stitch pattern.

The type of hook used—wood, plastic or metal—will influence gauge, so crochet your swatch with the hook you plan to use for the project. Try different hook sizes until your sample measures the required number of stitches and rows. To get fewer stitches to the inch/cm, use a larger hook; to get more stitches to the inch/cm, use a smaller hook.

It's a good idea to keep your gauge swatch in order to test blocking and cleaning methods.

GRANNY SQUARE BASICS

GRANNY SQUARE

(multi-color)

Ch 4. Join ch with a sl st forming a ring.

Rnd 1 (RS) Ch 3 (always counts as 1 dc), work 2 dc over ring, ch 2, * work 3 dc over ring, ch 2; rep from * 3 times. Join rnd with a sl st in 3rd ch of ch-3. Fasten off. From WS, join next color with a sl st in any ch-2 sp.

Rnd 2 Ch 3, work 2 dc in same ch-2 sp, ch 1, * work (3 dc, ch 2, 3 dc) in next ch-2 sp, ch 1; rep from * 3 times, end with 3 dc in beg ch-2 sp, ch 2. Join rnd with a sl st in 3rd ch of ch-3. Fasten off. From RS, join next color with a sl st in any ch-2 sp.

Rnd 3 Ch 3, work 2 dc in same ch-2 sp, ch 1, * work 3 dc in next ch-1 sp, ch 1, work (3 dc, ch 2, 3 dc) in next ch-2 sp, ch 1; rep from * 3 times, end with 3 dc in next ch-1 sp, ch 1, 3 dc in beg ch-2 sp, ch 2. Join rnd with a sl st in 3rd ch of ch-3. Fasten off. From WS, join next color with a sl st in any ch-2 sp.

Rnd 4 Ch 3, work 2 dc in same ch-2 sp, ch 1, * [work 3 dc in next ch-1 sp, ch 1] twice, work (3 dc, ch 2, 3 dc) in next ch-2 sp, ch 1; rep from * 3 times, end with [work 3 dc in next ch-1 sp, ch 1] twice, 3 dc in beg ch-2 sp, ch 2. Join rnd with a sl st in 3rd ch of ch-3. Fasten off. From RS, join next color with a sl st in any ch-2 sp.

Rnd 5 Ch 3, work 2 dc in same ch-2 sp, ch 1, * [work 3 dc in next ch-1 sp, ch 1] 3 times, work (3 dc, ch 2, 3 dc) in next ch-2 sp, ch 1; rep from * 3 times, end with [work 3 dc in next ch-1 sp, ch 1] 3 times, 3 dc in beg ch-2 sp, ch 2. Join rnd with a sl st in 3rd ch of ch-3. Fasten off leaving a long tail for sewing.

GRANNY SQUARE

(solid color)

Ch 4. Join ch with a sl st forming a ring.

Rnd 1 (RS) Ch 3 (always counts as 1 dc), work 2 dc over ring, ch 1, * work 3 dc over ring, ch 1; rep from * 3 times. Join rnd with a

BLANKET STITCH

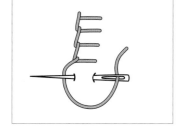

CHAIN STITCH

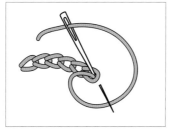

RUNNING STITCH

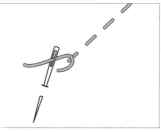

SATIN STITCH

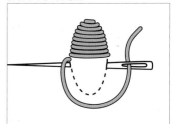

sl st in 3rd ch of ch-3. Turn.

Rnd 2 Ch 3, work (2 dc, ch 2, 3dc) in first ch-1 sp, ch 1, * work (3 dc, ch 1, 3 dc) in next ch-1 sp, ch 1; rep from * 3 times. Join rnd with a sl st in 3rd ch of ch-3. Fasten off leaving a long tail for sewing.

HALF-GRANNY

(multi-color)

Ch 3. Join ch with a sl st formng a ring.

Row 1 (RS) Ch 4 (counts as 1 dc and ch-1), work (3 dc, ch 2, 3 dc) over ring, ch 1, dc over ring, joining next color. Ch 3, turn.

Row 2 Work 3 dc in first ch-1 sp, ch 1, work (3 dc, ch 2, 3 dc) in ch-2 sp, ch 1, work 3 dc in last ch-1 sp. Fasten off leaving a long tail for sewing.

HALF-GRANNY

(solid color)

Ch 3. Join ch with a sl st formng a ring.

Row 1 (RS) Ch 4 (counts as 1 dc and ch-1), work (3 dc, ch 2, 3 dc) over ring, ch 1, dc over ring. Ch 3, turn.

Row 2 Work 3 dc in first ch-1 sp, ch 1, work (3 dc, ch 2, 3 dc) in ch-2 sp, ch 1, work 3 dc in last ch-1 sp. Fasten off leaving a long tail for sewing.

QUARTER-GRANNY

(solid color)

Ch 3. Join ch with a sl st formng a ring.

Row 1 (RS) Ch 3 (counts as 1 dc), work (2 dc, ch 2, 3 dc) over ring. Fasten off leaving a long tail for sewing.

BLOCKING

Blocking is a crucial finishing step in the crocheting process. It is the best way to shape pattern pieces and smooth crocheted edges in preparation for sewing together. Most designs retain their shape if the blocking stages in the instructions are followed carefully. Choose a blocking method according to the instructions on the yarn care label, and when in doubt, test-block your gauge swatch.

Wet Block Method

Using rust-proof pins, pin pieces to measurements on a flat surface and lightly dampen using a spray bottle. Allow to dry before removing pins.

Steam Block Method

With wrong sides facing, pin pieces. Steam lightly, holding the iron 2"/5cm above the piece. Do not press or it will flatten stitches.

CARE

Refer to the yarn label for the recommended cleaning method. Many of the projects in the book can be washed either by hand or in the machine on a gentle or wool cycle using lukewarm water with a mild detergent. Do not agitate or soak for more than 10 minutes. Rinse gently with tepid water, then fold in a towel and gently press the water out. Lay flat to dry, away from excess heat and light. Check the yarn label for any specific care instructions such as dry cleaning or tumble drying.

CROCHETING GLOSSARY

decrease 1 dc [Yo. Insert hook into next st and draw up a lp. Yo and draw through 2 lps] twice, yo and draw through all 3 lps on hook.

decrease 1 hdc [Yo, insert hook into next st and draw up a lp] twice, yo and draw through all 5 lps on hook.

decrease 1 sc [Insert hook into next st and draw up a lp] twice, yo and draw through all 3 lps on hook.

increase 1 stitch Work 2 sts in 1 st.

join yarn with a dc Make a slip knot, then yo. Insert hook into st. Yo and draw up a lp. [Yo and draw through 2 lps on hook] twice.

join yarn with a hdc Make a slip knot, then yo. Insert hook into st. Yo and draw up a lp. Yo and draw through 3 lps on hook.

join yarn with a sc Make a slip knot. Insert hook into st. Yo and draw up a lp. Yo and draw through 2 lps on hook.

join yarn with a sl st Make a slip knot. Insert hook into st. Yo and draw up a lp and draw through lp on hook.

STEM STITCH

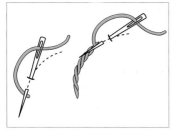

STRAIGHT STITCH

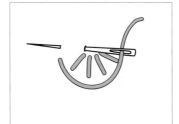

CROCHET ABBREVIATIONS

approx approximately

beg begin(ning)

CC contrasting color

ch chain(s)

cont continu(e)(ing)

dc double crochet (UK: tr treble)

dec decrease(ing) (see glossary)

g gram(s)

hdc half double crochet (UK: htr half treble)

inc increas(e)(ing) (see glossary)

lp(s) loop(s)

m meter(s)

mm millimeter(s)

MC main color

oz ounce(s)

pat(s) pattern(s)

rem remain(s)(ing)

rep repeat

rnd(s) round(s)

RS right side(s)

sc single crochet (UK: dc double crochet)

sk skip

sl slip

sl st slip st (UK: sc single crochet)

st(s) stitch(es)

tog together

tr treble crochet (UK: dtr double treble)

WS wrong side(s)

yd yard(s)

yo yarn over

* = repeat directions following * as many times as indicated

[ ] = repeat directions inside brackets as many times as indicated

( ) = work directions contained inside parentheses in st indicated

FRINGE

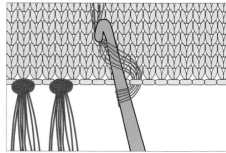

Simple fringe: Cut yarn twice desired length plus extra for knotting. On wrong side, insert hook from front to back through piece and over folded yarn. Pull yarn through. Draw ends through and tighten. Trim yarn.

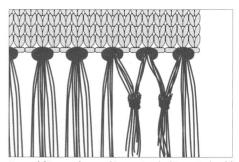

Knotted fringe: After working a simple fringe (it should be longer to allow for extra knotting), take one half of the strands from each fringe and knot them with half the strands from the neighboring fringe.

MAKING POMPOMS

POMPOM TEMPLATE

1

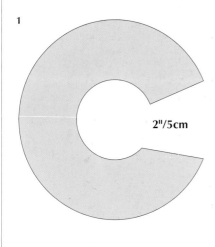

2"/5cm

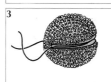

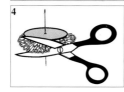

1 Following the template, cut two circular pieces of cardboard.

2 Place tie strand between the circles. Wrap yarn around circles. Cut between circles.

3 Knot tie strand tightly. Remove cardboard.

4 Place pompom between 2 smaller cardboard circles held together with a long needle and trim edges.

Note: For the safety and protection of your child, it is important to secure all pompoms and bobbles to the baby garment design. We recommend firmly tugging each pompom and bobble after each one is sewn on to ensure that they're secure.